THE IDEA FACTORY

THE IDEA
FACTORY

A guide to more creative
thinking and writing

Valerie Parv

ALLEN & UNWIN

Cover concept, Paul Parv
Illustration p viii, Richard Collins
All other illustrations, Paul Parv

First published in 1995 by
Allen & Unwin
9 Atchison Street, St Leonards, NSW 2065 Australia
Phone: (61 2) 9901 4088
Fax: (61 2) 9906 2218
E-mail: frontdesk@allen-unwin.com.au
URL: http://www.allen-unwin.com.au

National Library of Australia
Cataloguing-in-Publication entry:

Parv, Valerie.
  The idea factory: a guide to more creative thinking and
  writing.

  Bibliography.
  Includes index.
  ISBN 1 86373 918 1.

  1. Creative writing—Handbooks, manuals, etc. 2. Creative
  thinking—Handbooks, manuals, etc. 3. Thought and thinking.

  I. Title.

153.35

Set in 11/12.5 pt Bembo by DOCUPRO, Sydney
Printed by Australian Print Group, Maryborough, Victoria.

10 9 8 7 6 5 4 3 2

For Nicholas and Amelia Lawrence,
the creators of the future

Contents

"You've torn your left hemisphere. Did you warm up before thinking?"

Preface

Thinking is the ultimate human resource.
Edward de Bono
de Bono's Thinking Course

For too long creativity has been treated as the province of a gifted few, but I believe it is within reach of most people. You have only to watch a child playing 'pretend' to realise that the ability to visualise, to 'put two and two together and get six' is latent in almost everyone. But as we grow up we let this precious resource atrophy until we convince ourselves it was never there in the first place.

The drive to create is a powerful one, as I found when I developed my home study course in romance writing, later published as *The Art of Romance Writing*. This course put me in touch with thousands of people who shared a common goal: to write a successful romantic novel. For many it was their first attempt at realising a long-held dream to write. For others it was a new direction. But for all of them it was an adventure in creativity which I was privileged to share.

Many of those students are now published in various fields, but even those who may never publish have shared the joy—the *sanuk*, as it's known in Thailand—of playing 'let's pretend' as adults. Now they're back in touch with their creative abilities, I hope they will never again let them slip out of use.

Creativity is a tool not only for writers but for everyone

who wants a more fulfilling life. Paul Keating acknowledged this in his 1994 Cultural Policy Statement when he said '. . . the more we succeed in encouraging a creative spirit and the flow of creative ideas, the more we will succeed as an economy and society.'

Not everyone sees creativity as 'real' work. Samuel Goldwyn was said to prowl the corridors of MGM Studios listening for the sound of typewriters tapping. He paid the writers to write, not to think, he stated. But how can you write if you can't think? What do you write about? That's where this book comes in. Among my writing students I noticed a kind of shyness towards ideas, as if they could bite.

They can't.

But they *can* enrich, excite and challenge, if only they are let off their leashes and given full rein. Only then can you discover what heights you are capable of scaling using your newfound creativity muscle.

Scaling heights is the analogy used by the writer and music producer, Ian Chambers, who likens writing to high-diving. 'You practise your craft until you are ready to take the big plunge. And, in the end, it's just you up there on that platform.'

Some of the themes in this book were first explored in my column, 'A writer's lot', in *The Australian Writers' News*, sadly now defunct. I hope it wasn't something I said! However, the many positive responses to these columns convinced me that there is a need for a book which not only gives writers permission to explore their creativity to the full, but shows how it can be done and how enjoyable the results can be.

Much of this material has been road-tested in workshops I've conducted around Australia, and I wish to thank those students for their invaluable input. As always, the list of people deserving thanks is long and doubtless incomplete, but thank you anyway. In particular I thank Des Theodore, Trisha Sunholm, Barry Watts and Sandy Coghlan for their unique contributions, acknowledged where I have shamelessly plundered their ideas (don't worry, there are lots more where they came from!). To the staff of Macquarie University Library and the members of the many writing groups including Pegasus, The Society of Women Writers NSW and the Romance Writers of Australia. To fellow writers Helen Bianchin, Angela Devine, Robyn Donald, Frank and Wendy Brennan, Marion Lennox and Lyn Howard, who lead so superbly by example. Sadly, Frank Brennan passed away earlier this year but his vast body of work and indomitable spirit will continue to inspire all who knew him. Also thank you to my agent, Linda Tate, for her encouragement and support, as well as to Louise Shortus, Dr Denis Waitley, Lawrence Block and the late Gene Roddenberry, who inspired me more than they can know. Finally, my heartfelt appreciation to my husband Paul, whose drawings enrich the text, and to my parents Arthur and Elizabeth Newsum, who believed in my creativity before I did. As these pages reveal, belief is half the battle.

May the resource be with you.

Valerie Parv
Sydney 1995

1

The importance of ideas

You want to write but where do you start? How do you generate that glimmer of original thought which becomes an exciting non-fiction piece, short story or novel? How do you come up with something fresh and new to say when so much has already been written?

How do you get started when your mind is as blank as the paper in front of you?

How do you develop characters who come to life on the page?

In short, where do you get your ideas?

Ideas on demand

Every writer is asked this question at some time, and there are as many answers as there are writers. The American novelist and teacher Lawrence Block tried telling people that he subscribed to *The Ideas Book*, a magazine filled with plot ideas from which writers could pick and choose. Having selected an idea, they could reserve it and develop a story around it. The trouble with this nonsense is that people believed it and started asking how they could become subscribers.

The Australian writer Des Theodore interprets the question to mean not only 'Where do you get your grand flash of vision?' but also 'How do you sustain it while putting a book together?' In other words, how do you turn a pile of blank pages into a book?

However it is interpreted, the question still begs an answer. Where do ideas come from? Can you be taught how to have them? Because without that initial spark there is no point developing the rest of the story or book. It will have little of original value to recommend it.

My opinion, gained through writing 50 books of my own, teaching workshops up to university level and reading the work of hundreds of students, is that there *are* techniques you can learn that will enable you to have workable ideas on demand. They will also sustain you throughout a long project and help you to overcome most writing blocks.

In my view, most of the limitations placed on creativity are self-imposed. This is good news because it means you have the power to change how you think about your own creativity and become what Dr Wayne Dyer calls a 'no-limit person'. Once you discover how to apply the straightforward techniques described in this book you will have more ideas than you've ever had before, and they will almost certainly be more original.

Now here's the bad news.

These techniques won't automatically turn you into a best-selling writer. It is still up to you to learn and apply the techniques of good writing. Learn how to use words to best advantage; how to hook and hold readers and pull them through the pages of your work so they forget everything else. Make them miss their stops on the train. Boil the dinner dry. Good writing can do all of this—and almost incidentally earn its creator a place in literary history.

There are dozens of helpful books from which you can learn basic writing techniques. You should aim to build up a library of such works and refer to them often. Joining writers' organisations and workshop groups is another good way to hone your technique. But I can tell you this: learning writing techniques is the easy part. Ideas are much more elusive.

As a teacher of writing I spent a couple of years appraising hundreds of book proposals by students from five countries. All but a handful of the proposals were fluently written and well presented. With only two exceptions, what they lacked above all was *originality*.

The majority lacked good underlying ideas which made me want to read on to find out how they were resolved.

They lacked a fresh approach.

They told me nothing new.

The writers had spent so much time polishing their prose and worrying about the widths of their margins that they forgot one vital principle: books are about new ideas. The very word 'novel' comes from the Latin *novus*—new.

First things first

Imagine hearing this comment at your next cocktail party: 'Darling, I loved your book. The margins were stunningly wide and the spelling was simply flawless. I've never seen such spectacular typing in my life.'

Such a conversation seems preposterous, yet many writers agonise over these details and forget the main purpose for writing a story—to take the reader on a voyage of discovery.

Years ago I attended a writers' meeting at which an hour was spent arguing over whether the entries in a short story competition should be fastened with pins or paper clips.

Frequently I'm asked what sort of computer or word processor I use, as if it matters. One would-be writer actually observed, 'If I had a machine like yours I could write successful books too'.

If this were true, then every cook with a supply of flour, water, eggs and butter would be a great chef. Yet, as everyone who eats in restaurants knows, there are cooks and there are chefs. It's all in how the ingredients are used.

My first book was written on an ancient manual typewriter purchased for $25 from a trash and treasure market. The machine was sheer drudgery to use and as soon as I secured a contract for my second book I traded up to a portable electric typewriter. It was fun to operate but much too lightweight, not being designed as an office machine. It was more suited to typing letters or student homework, so it tended to break down a lot.

Gradually with each writing success I upgraded to a better machine, until today I use what's called an 'intelligent typewriter', which has a working memory and a disk drive. The only difference between it and a computer is the size of the screen, and this is purely a personal preference. Some day I'll invest in a full-screen computer—but it will have no effect whatsoever on the quality of my writing.

It's no accident that the programs for writers are called *word processing* software. No matter how sophisticated they are, that's all they do—process the words *you* create.

Garbage in, garbage out

Remember the famous computer term GIGO. It stands for 'garbage in, garbage out' and is never more appropriate than when applied to creative writing. What you get out of any machine depends on what you put in.

4

There are probably already programs in existence designed to produce a piece of fiction from combinations of characters and plot fragments, but the elements will still have to be programmed into the machine in the first place. GIGO.

However sophisticated it is, the machine on which you write is only a tool to make the *processing* of the words easier and more efficient. Getting the ideas is still up to you. As best-selling romance writer Emma Darcy expresses it, 'all the words you need are to be found in the dictionary. All you have to do is put them in the right order.'

Equally, no good manuscript was ever rejected because of narrow margins, single spacing or even for being handwritten and barely legible, otherwise such works as Albert Facey's *A Fortunate Life* would never have been published. Neither would *Gone With the Wind*, which is said to have been

"If I had a chisel like Rodin's,
I could be a great sculptor, too."

submitted in a large box, the disarranged sheets including several drafts of some pages.

In its guidelines to authors, romance publishers Harlequin Mills & Boon say, 'surprisingly we don't worry too much about flawless presentation; a book that has been written with genuine feeling can be forgiven a few typing mistakes. What is more important is a love of storytelling combined with *a freshness and originality of approach* . . . an individual touch . . . [the author's] particular way of telling a story, this quality is vital' (italics added).

This doesn't mean you can get away with sloppy presentation. In these competitive times, a manuscript needs every advantage, including clean printing, a compelling title, and presentation that meets publishing industry requirements.

But you must get your priorities right.

Every publisher, even those who don't normally read unsolicited material, still passionately seeks that 'fresh and original approach' and genuine love of storytelling.

What they seek are exciting new ideas.

Manner versus matter

The veteran science fiction writer Theodore Sturgeon says that good writing depends on both matter and manner. Manner, he says, is the way the story is told. Excellence in manner will sell stories and may even get you known as a good writer. But gloss and polish alone won't make you a great or important writer because, like soap bubbles, you leave nothing of value behind.

According to Sturgeon, readers want *matter* for their money. They don't want tracts and manuals. They want content which will move them, ignite their passions, share visions, joys and terrors as well as knowledge.

If you put powerful ideas into your writing you will be forgiven quite substantial technical flaws. A good example is Clive Cussler's *Raise the Titanic*. This book is riddled with irritating writing flaws, such as the writer changing from one viewpoint character to another, sometimes several times within one paragraph. I found this most disconcerting. But along with millions of other readers, I couldn't put the book down. I simply had to know what would happen when the *Titanic* was raised from its watery grave. What would they find? Would the characters be prevented from reaching their goal?

The writer hooked me with a compelling idea which no-one else had explored. His expert knowledge of the world of undersea diving gave the book a sense of realism which was irresistible. But most of all, he was obviously so committed to the central idea of the novel that his passion shone through the pages. Presumably this was what caught the eye of the editor who first read the manuscript.

Such is the power of an idea. It can overcome the odds of the so-called slush pile, that graveyard of unsolicited manuscripts to be found in every publisher's office. It can keep overworked editors awake half the night and send them to acquisitions meetings in a fever of determination to have their firm acquire the book.

So it is here you would do well to concentrate your efforts, for I truly believe that ideas are what separate the merely competent writers from the potential best-sellers.

Your own idea factory

Too often we're told that creativity is the province of a gifted few. In fact practically everyone possesses a built-in idea factory which can be fine-tuned once you know the secrets.

Turning on the flow of ideas is perfectly possible once you master some of the skills described in this book. You will also discover step-by-step ways to come up with wild possibilities, then tame them into workable ideas.

We'll investigate the most common reasons why the ideas dry up, showing you how to overcome blocks such as fear of failure.

Concepts such as the ice-ball theory should reassure you sufficiently to dare almost any new idea. It's like having a guarantee that you can't fail.

Why you need ideas

The publishing world is becoming increasingly competitive. One London publisher states that for every 5000 manuscripts it receives every year, it does well to accept ten. Magazines are inundated with short story manuscripts when there are only a handful of slots open to them each month.

The world itself is becoming increasingly complex, with ever more information to be assimilated and problems to be solved. Just as ideas will make your writing stand out from the crowd, ideas are what will solve the world's problems. In *Future Shock*, Alvin Toffler points out that we need more imagination to chart our future as human beings. He says conjecture, speculation and visionary views are as necessary now as feet-on-the-floor realism has been up to this point. For this reason, some of the world's biggest companies are hiring futurists and science fiction writers as consultants, not to provide scientific forecasts but to indulge in mind-stretching speculation.

As far back as 1972, Helen Jean Burn, head writer for the Maryland Centre for Public Broadcasting, acknowledged this development, among other issues, when she wrote:

> There is something in the creative process which enables perceptive minds to reach beyond the senses into truths not yet uncovered and further, to translate those truths into terms ordinary people can understand, become prepared for, and in time learn to live with.

Or, as Sigmund Freud put it, 'Every time we scientists think we have made a discovery we find some poet has been there centuries before us.'

Toffler forecasts the setting up of Imaginetic Centres, where creative people will get together to speculate about possible future trends for the good of society. They might look at new ways to deal with problems such as noise pollution, an aging population and others.

According to Toffler, the ideal creative person is willing to play the fool and toy with the absurd, only later subjecting the stream of ideas to critical judgment. This process has become known as *brainstorming*, and later we'll look at specific methods writers can use to brainstorm ideas either alone or in supportive groups.

Even if only a fraction of the ideas thus produced survive the critical process, they are still vitally important, whether they're intended to improve your writing or solve the world's problems.

Why be creative?

You can't see it, touch it or smell it. Yet without it we have far fewer resources for dealing with life's problems. And the 'perceptive mind' which reaches for 'truths not yet uncovered' would have no tools with which to uncover those truths, far less be able to translate them into terms readers can understand and relate to.

9

Lawrence Block calls writing 'telling lies for fun and profit'. However lucrative the profit part, it's a fact that best-selling writers keep writing even after having made huge fortunes. Even those who swear that they will never again touch pen or keyboard are soon driven to developing plots and spinning tales.

Why?

The first part of Block's maxim might hold the key. Writing is probably the best fun you can have with your clothes on. What other occupation pays its practitioners, sometimes handsomely, for telling lies? Sure it's a solitary occupation and frequently frustrating in the extreme, especially when the going gets tough, as it does for every writer at times. In the section on pulling out the stops, we'll look at ways to handle these tough times. But it's also hugely rewarding, and not always in money terms.

The English author Keith Waterhouse lamented:

> If you were to tell me that of the next hundred-plus articles and stories I write, less than half a dozen will ever see publication, and that my earnings from writing this year will amount to no more than £2, next year to nothing at all and the year after to £12, I should probably take up selling used cars instead.

Yet that was his track record for his first three years as a writer, and he kept on writing.

In the southern hemisphere, the situation he describes is exacerbated by much smaller markets and competition from other English-speaking countries.

So why do writers persist against such odds? For most writers there isn't any choice. Despite Samuel Johnson's assertion that only blockheads write other than for money, lack of commercial success has never stopped a writer from writing.

Many have resorted to self-publishing, including William Blake, Robert Burns, Edgar Allen Poe, Mark Twain and James Joyce. The famous writer's guide *The Elements of Style* was originally self-published. Other writers, among them Honoré de Balzac and Alexandre Dumas, survived by taking commissions so they could keep on writing, sometimes producing their best works under financial duress.

The importance of attitude

The Australian author Jo Beaumont says that what matters is the writer's attitude to the craft, and his or her ability to practise it effectively, whatever form it takes (short stories, articles, novels) and whatever we choose to call it (authorship, journalism).

The New Zealand author Margaret Mahy, who has written more than 40 books, said in an interview with Duncan Ball in *The Australian Author* that at first, she wrote everything everyone asked her to. Her output included TV writing, instructional readers and trade books. When it came to publicising her work, she said, she was 'an entertainer, a publicist and a jack-of-all-trades'. While she described her promotional efforts as 'a cheap level of self-advertisement' she admitted to enjoying it, despite being a serious writer at heart. 'As well as putting on a wig and singing out of tune, I write into the small hours of the morning.'

This is the voice of dedication. I groan when people tell me they have decided to 'take up' writing in their later years or as a hobby. In my experience writing takes *you* up and

11

doesn't put you down until you head for that great library in the sky.

Most writers are driven by the urge to write as soon as they can hold a pen. I wrote before I knew what a writer was. My first poem was published on the children's page of a Sunday newspaper when I was seven. My first book, *The Bush Trekkers*, was written in pencil in an exercise book when I was nine.

So, you know if you have the drive to write because it has already expressed itself in similar ways. You are aware of the need to learn your craft by taking courses, joining workshops and groups and reading books about writing technique. The next question is where this book comes in. What do you write *about*?

What's your theme?

All good writing must be about something—Sturgeon's matter. The something is the idea which prompts you to put it down in the first place. This doesn't mean preaching or writing what publishers call issues books disguised as fiction. By all means explore issues in journalistic form, but in fiction, leave it to your characters to express their own points of view. As they say in Hollywood, 'If you've got a message, send it Western Union.'

The matter you write about will later be identified as your theme, and generally it isn't discernible even by the author until many words are on the page. Suddenly you discover that you've written a novel exploring the effects of divorce on different members of the same family, or you've highlighted the problems dislocation causes to children. It's better if you don't try to define your theme at the outset.

Instead, aim to create interesting, believable characters with real problems and conflicts to resolve among themselves, and the theme will grow of its own accord. It is all the more powerful when it is 'shown' through the characters rather than being 'told' by the author.

As a writer you have extraordinary tools at your disposal, and this is where the fun comes in. It's the truly creative stage, when anything is possible. You are free to imagine any town, city or universe you like, people it with whomever you choose, dictate the manner of their lives and even their deaths. As medical writer, Marion Lennox, told me with some relish, 'I love a good death'.

In the real world, things go wrong without rhyme or reason. Bad things happen to good people. Saints fall ill with terminal diseases while sinners go right on sinning in perfect health. Whatever your beliefs, these things often defy explanation. But the writer can right all the wrongs, redress the injustices, reward the virtuous and punish what Leslie Charteris called 'the ungodly' in any manner your imagination can conceive.

It's a heady ability and I suspect one of the main reasons why writing is so addictive, whether you make enough money to retire on or never earn a cent from your work.

Does it have sanuk?

In Thailand, there's a tendency to judge the value of an endeavour by the amount of *sanuk* it contains. The word roughly translates as 'fun'. Anything not *sanuk* is not considered worth pursuing.

This book aims to put the *sanuk* back into your thinking and your writing. Forget all those quotations about sitting down at the keyboard and opening a vein. For me the best kind of writing, whether it's a business memo or a blockbuster novel, comes from the creative right brain. We'll examine right-brain thinking and how to tap into it later in the book but for now, accept that your right brain is the side having all the *sanuk*.

Your left brain is the editor and critic, and unfortunately it's the part that remains in charge most of the time. The world we live in is a complex and daunting place. Yet putting more reliance on the technically inclined left brain is not going to get us through. As Alvin Toffler points out, we need *more* creativity, *more* right-brain thinking to help us deal with what's ahead.

Think of our cave-dwelling ancestors. At some stage the hunters were faced with starvation from dwindling game and unreliable food supplies. The left-brain solution was to hunt more and for longer periods, ranging further and further afield. Then some right-brain thinker sat down and looked at things a different way. The problem wasn't so much how to find the game as how to ensure a reliable food supply. (Being able to zero in on the exact problem to be solved is a hallmark of creative thinking which we'll examine in more detail later.) Having identified the problem—providing a reliable food supply—the right-brained cave dweller decided to try to grow food in one spot and corral a few game animals close to home rather than chase after them endlessly. Agriculture was on the way to being invented.

No doubt that First Farmer had to endure a lot of nagging from the left-brained members of his tribe who would have pointed out all the reasons why his idea wouldn't work. A perceptive few, whom Napoleon Hill has termed the

"This gardening stuff will
never catch on, you know."

'mastermind group', might be open to possibilities and willing
to try new things.

In which group do you think you would find your own
ancestors? I hope mine were among the First Farmer's group,
or at least among the possibility seekers.

But as you'll find out when we look at the idea-generating
techniques of brainstorming and clustering, the doomsayers are
usually in the majority. Sometimes they're even inside your
own head. The trick is to learn how to win out over them
because, like the poor of biblical fame, they are always with us.

The need for change

An organisation called the Club of Rome, made up of
representatives of national governments and individuals

15

concerned with future trends, identified the need for a change in thinking to help deal with the increasing complexity and speed of change in the world. It called for a change from maintenance learning to innovative learning. This was supported by Australia's Commission for the Future. In a report released in 1989, it said the days when formal learning finished at school are over: we need to develop learning habits which continue throughout life.

Innovative learning deals not only with the absorption of facts and precedents but also with conjecture and speculation—the realm of ideas. Innovative learning emphasises the elements needed to anticipate and deal with changes in every area of life, especially values, human relations and images.

In *No Limits to Learning* (Pergamon Press 1979), James Botkin, Mahdi Elmandjra and Mircea Malitza divide innovative learning into two facets: anticipation and participation.

Anticipation is the capacity to face new situations, deal with the future and consider coming events and possible consequences. Imagination plays a key part in anticipation, although it can also be analytical and data based. Using the tools of conjecture, hypothesis and simulation, we can forecast the implications of our present-day activities. This is the sociological equivalent of what science fiction writers do when they ask 'What if . . .?' and 'If this goes on . . .'.

Innovative learning also calls for participation. It won't be good enough to leave all the decision making and planning to higher authorities. At present there's a tendency to have 'participation by veto'. We protest when we *don't* want something to happen. A more creative approach is to seek out what we *do* want; to become active rather than reactive. This books sets out to give you some methods that make this not only possible but, I hope, pleasurable—with the required amount of *sanuk*.

The hallmarks of creativity

Like the crops and animals of our cave-dwelling ancestors, creativity can be 'domesticated' through innovative learning so it becomes a tool you can call up and use on demand.

Just as farming took the hit-and-miss out of finding enough food to survive, you can 'tame' creativity so that imagination and intuition are available to you whenever you need them.

According to the psychologist Dr Denis Waitley, there are several characteristics which identify the creative person. If you don't possess these qualities now, you can start putting innovative learning to work for you and seek ways to develop them in yourself. They include:

- optimism about the future
- discontent with the status quo
- curiosity and skill in observation
- the ability to daydream and fantasise
- an adventurous outlook and interest in many subjects
- the ability to recognise and break bad habits
- independent thinking

Creative people are able to use both the right and left sides of the brain in order to put ideas (right-brained in origin) into action (left-brained in execution).

There's another important quality shared by creative people. They *believe* they are creative. Either they've never been told they aren't creative or if so, they have chosen to believe otherwise.

Which brings us to the important contributions trust and belief make to the output of your idea factory.

In a nutshell

1 Most limitations on creativity are self-imposed. You *can* learn to have good ideas on demand.
2 The quality of your writing depends on the power and originality of your ideas—garbage in, garbage out.
3 Matter (what you have to say) is more important than manner (how you say it).
4 Ideas are becoming increasingly important, not only in writing but to help us deal with life's problems in the real world.
5 Your attitude to writing influences your progress. Does the work provide you with *sanuk* (fun)?
6 Do you have, or will you cultivate, these qualities of creative people: optimism, curiosity, an adventurous outlook, wide-ranging interests, the ability to recognise and correct bad habits, discontent with the status quo, and a liking for independent thinking?

2

Believing is seeing

How much difference can belief make to the number and kind of ideas you are able to have? You'd be surprised. Think of the little girl in kindergarten. Along with her classmates, she was asked to draw a picture with her crayons, so she got to work busily. After a while the teacher went around the class and asked the children what they had drawn. One little boy had drawn a house with two big front windows and a red front door. Another girl had drawn herself playing with her puppy. But the third little girl was still hard at work, her tongue protruding slightly from the side of her mouth as she concentrated fiercely. When asked what she was so intent on drawing, without looking up she said, 'I'm drawing God'.

The teacher was taken aback and said as gently as she could, 'But dear, nobody knows what God looks like'.

The little girl kept drawing and said firmly, 'They will in a minute'.

This little girl had no doubt at all that she could produce a reasonable likeness no matter what anybody else thought. She *believed* she could do it, so nothing could stop her.

So it is with creativity. For far too long we've subscribed to the notion that to be 'creative' one must be somehow 'gifted'. However, creativity is being accepted more and more as a learnable skill. All of the qualities Dr Denis Waitley attributes to creative people can be developed in yourself with a little effort.

How hard can it be to decide to be optimistic about the future, to be curious about the world around you and skilful in observing it, to be interested in many subjects, to decide to think for yourself and, most pleasurable of all, to let yourself daydream and fantasise? None of these abilities is inborn. They are all learnable and *sanuk* to work on.

Somebody once said that if you believe you can or if you believe you can't, you're right. Whichever you decide to believe will turn out to be true. There's nothing mysterious or metaphysical about this. The more you tell yourself that you're clumsy or forgetful, the more your brain gets the message 'be clumsy' or 'be forgetful'. It's a kind of persistent programming which takes root in your subconscious over time, until you start to act in accordance with this programming.

The writing teacher Barry Watts advises his students to send a different kind of message to themselves. When you drop something, forget something or otherwise behave in a way you find unsatisfactory, he says, don't berate yourself for the failing. Instead, tell yourself, 'That's not like me. Next time I'll . . .' and turn the message you send to your subconscious into a positive one.

Accentuate the positive

On a visit to Australia some years ago, Dr Denis Waitley told me of an experience that illustrates how easy it is to give the subconscious the wrong message. Asked to help a retail store deal with a rise in shoplifting, he arranged to have a message broadcast under some music. The message was 'don't shoplift, don't shoplift'. The incidence of shoplifting actually increased because the message planted the idea in the shoppers' minds.

They didn't absorb the 'don't' part but only the 'shoplift' part. When the message was changed to 'please pay at the door', things began to improve.

You can practise giving positive messages to yourself and others almost every day. Instead of telling a family member 'Don't forget the bread', try saying 'Remember to buy the bread'. That way their subconscious will hear 'remember the bread' instead of 'forget the bread'. You can also do this with the messages you give yourself. Try to phrase reminders in a positive way so that 'Don't forget to call the client' becomes 'Remember to call the client'.

Similarly, if your writing involves setting out instructions or guidelines for how to do something, try to phrase them in a positive way. When you think about it, it's amazing how much time we spend telling people what we *don't* want them to do, and how comparatively little on what we *do* want from them. A poster I saw on a nursing home wall sums it up perfectly: 'Don't tell me what I'm doing wrong, tell me what I'm doing right.'

New ways of seeing

Betty Edwards, well known for her book *Drawing on the Right Side of the Brain*, describes the task of releasing our creative potential as a two-step process. First we need to get rid of the concept that only a few talented people can be creative. Then we need to focus on what we tell ourselves and how we order that information.

Edwards teaches people to draw by showing them new ways of seeing that 'guide strategies in creative thinking and problem solving, just as, through learning to read, you acquire verbal knowledge'.

If asked to draw a picture, most people who aren't artists of some kind will say something like, 'Oh, but I have no skill/talent/gift for drawing.' This belief gets in the way of reality. Simply by helping people to change that belief, Betty Edwards has taught people to draw who didn't believe they could draw a line.

One of her most effective exercises is to present students with an upside-down picture and ask them to resist the temptation to look at it right side up. They are asked to copy the picture upside down, concentrating on the lines and spaces rather than on what the picture is supposed to represent.

I've tried this exercise and it works astonishingly well. The technique is described in detail in *Drawing on the Artist Within, How to Release Your Hidden Creativity* by Betty Edwards (Fontana, London 1987).

There's an upside-down picture on p.23 so you can try it for yourself. Start copying the picture from any point you like and concentrate only on the lines and spaces and their relationship to each other. Try to quiet the intellectual part of your brain, which is probably saying, 'This is a leg here and a knee there,' and just focus on the lines and spaces.

When you finish and turn both drawings right side up, you'll be surprised how good your effort will be. This is because drawing upside down forces you to 'see' the subject in a new way, free from the usual preconceptions that inhibit creativity.

In drawing as in thinking, sometimes it helps not to know what the end result is intended to look like. Starting with a finished product in mind can often blind you to your many options. Artists naturally see the relationship of lines, shadows and spaces rather than the entire object, and you can teach yourself to do the same.

Letting go of the needle

There are many stories that show how changing one's perceptions can result in breakthrough insights. One of the most famous concerns the inventor of the sewing machine, Elias Howe. As anyone who has ever sewn on a button knows, a needle has a point at one end and an eye at the other, through which the thread passes. To sew you pass the threaded needle through the material, pull it out the other side, and then push it back the opposite way. Faced with the need to attach the needle to his machine, Howe couldn't work out how to 'let go' of the needle so it could carry the thread through the fabric as happens when you sew by hand.

Unable to solve the problem through logical thinking Howe slept on it. This is often the best way to allow your creative right brain to work uninterrupted. Sure enough,

Howe had a dream in which he saw a tribe of savages carrying spears which had eye-shaped holes near the tips. During sleep, Howe's right brain had been able to look at the problem from a new angle, enabling him to see that the needle would work if it had the eye at the pointed end. Seeing in a new way enabled him to invent the sewing machine.

Drawing is a means of creative expression but it is also a means of creating understanding. As an advertising copywriter I used rough drawings to 'brief' an artist on how my writing worked with a visual concept. A rough drawing called a layout shows artists and photographers what is wanted from them. Leonardo da Vinci used drawings to study anatomy. Today manufacturers use drawings to guide purchasers in assembling new products. Sometimes they even work.

Think how many times drawings are used to get a message across, from road signs to identifying rest rooms. Drawings even cross language barriers. If you want to prohibit something, put the forbidden activity in a red circle with a red slash across it.

Draw the problem

Sometimes it helps to 'draw' a writing problem. Later we'll look at a technique called clustering, which is drawing of a different kind but still uses a visual approach to help you work out the structure of a writing project. As with road signs, visual images can stand for whole clusters of ideas and perceptions beyond words.

Just as looking at a picture upside down forces you to see in a new way, writing in a style other than your usual one is a good way to unblock your idea factory and generate new kinds of thinking.

All the words we use for creativity—inspiration, intuition, imagination, insight, vision, foresight—relate to *seeing*.

This is why it can help to come at a writing problem from a completely fresh angle, seeing it upside down as it were. If you have to write an article for an industry journal and can't get started, try drafting it as a poem or a play. Tom Wolfe drafted his articles as memos to his editor, who then printed the memos.

Romance writer Helen Bianchin says she often roughs out entire chapters of a novel in dialogue. This not only provides a change of perception but also helps to bring the characters to life, as they are forced to take on the whole job of telling the story. Later she fleshes out the chapter with narrative.

Faced with a character who seemed wooden and unconvincing, I wrote a few chapters of one book in the first person even though romance novels are generally written in the third person. Later I changed all the 'I' references to 'she'. With a few grammatical adjustments, the rest of the chapter remained as written and the character came to life much more effectively.

Change your method

You can also change perceptions by changing your method of working. If you usually work on a computer, try writing some of your project in long hand on a clipboard. Change the colour of the paper in accordance with the mood of the piece—pink for a romance novel, blue for science fiction, green for an environmental article, for example. In Hollywood, script changes are signalled by the addition of different-coloured sheets of paper. While this is intended to alert the cast and crew to the latest script changes, it also has the effect of making the script look more interesting, even if some scripts end up in all the colours of the rainbow.

Change your location

Writing in a different place can also bring about a change of perception and kick start your idea factory. A team of script-writers transferred their base of operations to the local McDonald's restaurant because the vivid yellow and red decor gave them a lift. In colour psychology terms, these are both 'energising' colours.

If your own working conditions don't energise you, try changing the colours around you and see if it helps. If you can't redecorate, try using brightly coloured throw rugs and curtains to achieve the same result.

Change your location.

26

The successful Australian novelist Robert G. Barrett, author of best-sellers such as *You Wouldn't Be Dead for Quids* and *White Shoes, White Lines and Blackie* writes in longhand on a clipboard at the beach, sitting on a banana lounge in his Speedos. His series hero, Les Norton, is an easy-going larrikin with an eye for beautiful women, so the atmosphere probably helps Robert to get into the mood of his stories. It's hard to imagine him achieving the same breezy style in a windowless office with grey walls.

This doesn't mean you need perfect surroundings in which to write successfully. Some of the world's greatest writing was produced under appalling conditions. As you'll see when we look at the different needs of right-brain and left-brain thinking, sometimes it is helpful to work in familiar surroundings, for only then is the critical left brain relaxed enough to let you indulge in truly creative thinking. The idea of changing your surroundings occasionally is simply to free yourself up, to let yourself 'see in a new way' so you are open to whatever inspiration you need.

There are other ways to change your working conditions to make it easier to generate new ideas. If you usually work on paper or on a screen, try talking the material into a tape recorder. Don't try to phrase things in any special way. Simply talk the material through as you would to a friend. You might find a surprising fluency in this approach, as Tom Wolfe did with his memos.

If talking into a tape recorder makes you feel self-conscious, and I should confess that it does for me, try writing out your material in point form. Don't be surprised if your 'points' gradually become more detailed until you're writing whole paragraphs. This is how I develop many of my own books. I begin with an outline in point form. Then, as I go down the page, the points become longer and longer until I'm throwing in bits of dialogue and narrative and the chapter is half written.

Write your thoughts

Instead of staring into space, try writing down your thoughts. This is nearly always effective because it keeps you focused and enables you to 'see' the material more objectively. As a by-product, it tells everyone else that you're working because they can hear the tap-tap of the keyboard. As somebody once said, the hardest thing for writers to do is convince others they're working when they're staring out the window.

Writing your thoughts can take any form you like. Explore the problem facing you in stream-of-consciousness style, for example: 'Well, let's see, I have two scenes here which are virtually the same. One is to show that my heroine has spent all the money the hero gave her, and not on what she told him she would . . . and the second is to show that she's gone and fallen in love with the hero. Could I combine them both into one scene? What if I have the hero confront the heroine with a bounced cheque and . . . wait a minute, I've got it . . . he accuses her of having an affair . . . what if he then thinks all bets are off and takes her to bed in the heat of the moment, which she wants anyway because now she knows she's in love with him . . .'

I used this technique to good effect when I was writing a 10,000-word novella for *The Australian Women's Weekly*. With a tight deadline I didn't have time to stare into space, so writing the problem out was the best way to solve it.

Writing your material in the form of a letter sometimes helps to get you going. Start off, 'Dear friend, I want to tell you about a writing project I have in mind. This will be a (book, article, story) about . . .' and go on to fill in the details. Make no attempt to edit what you say, just as you wouldn't edit a letter to a trusted friend. As soon as the idea starts to catch fire you can switch to a more conventional format.

Change your point of view

The ability to see things from more than one angle is crucial to a writer, but especially to a fiction writer. How can you create believable characters unless you can put yourself in another person's shoes?

This is a skill you can practise. Next time you read a news story about a crime, deliberately imagine yourself as the criminal. Do you feel remorse at your crime, or merely annoyance that you were caught? Do you blame someone else, the victim perhaps, for being foolish enough to provide you with the opportunity? Do you rationalise your actions so they make sense, at least to you? Can you justify them to yourself, and how? Would you do the same thing again or have you learned a lesson? How do you view the prospect of imprisonment? Have you been in prison before? If not, are you scared at the prospect, even if you present a brave front to others?

Now switch your perception to the victim of the crime. How do you feel now? Does the prospect of the criminal going to prison please you, vindicate you or sadden you at the waste of a human life? Has the crime affected the way you conduct your day-to-day life? Do you ask yourself 'why me?' or berate yourself for somehow inviting the crime? Is there something you could have done to change the outcome? What have you lost? What have you gained as a result of this experience? This last question may seem an odd one, but there is some good in practically every experience, even if it's only the resolve to be more cautious in future.

For the purpose of this exercise, you don't need to know anything about the real people or circumstances involved. It is merely designed to give you practice in 'seeing' both sides of a situation while putting yourself in another's place, even someone whose morality may be quite different from your own.

The signature test

In workshops I use another exercise to practise seeing the world from different points of view. The participants are asked to sign their names in the usual way at the top of a blank sheet of paper.

Underneath their normal signature I ask them to sign their name as a poor member of a religious order dedicated to prayer and self-sacrifice.

Finally they are asked to sign their name as a major Hollywood star who enjoys all the benefits and trappings of fame.

As you can imagine, the signature of the poor religious is invariably quite small and restrained compared with the person's usual signature. Some people even sign with an X to signify a lack of education or extreme humility. In contrast, the Hollywood signature is usually scrawling and flamboyant, taking up much more of the page and having lots of bold flourishes.

Try it yourself. Imagine how you would sign your name if you were:

- a weight lifter competing in the Olympic Games
- the Poet Laureate of England

- an Australian stockman
- an Antarctic explorer
- the captain of the Starship *Enterprise*

In our society we use the term 'seeing is believing'. I prefer Dr Wayne Dyer's version, used as the title of one of his books, *You'll See It When You Believe It.*

The fact that so much of our experience, from our religious beliefs to our ability to keep breathing while we sleep, has to be taken on trust, makes Dyer's version all the more accurate. You start with the belief, and then you see the reality. If you start by believing you can have as many ideas as you want when you want to, you will soon see the results.

Promise yourself only to think in positive terms for a fixed period, say a day. You'll be amazed how often you have to stop yourself and rephrase a negative thought in positive terms, because the habit of negativity is very strong. But it *can* be overcome with determination and practice, and the rewards are many.

The thought switch

Try this. Think of what you plan to do tomorrow. At exactly the same time, recall what you ate for your last meal. Unless you're a remarkable human being you'll be unable to think of both things at the same time. You will be more likely to switch back and forth between the two.

Now picture an animal, any animal. At the same time picture a tree in a park or garden. The same problem arises. You can't think of more than one thing at a time. This means you *can* control what you think about.

31

Since you can't hold a positive and a negative thought in your mind at the same time, any more than you can picture an animal and a tree simultaneously, you can switch off a negative thought as soon as you become aware of it. As soon as a negative thought starts to creep in, think the words 'switch off'. It helps to have a small, unobtrusive gesture to accompany the 'switch off' command. I use a tiny flick of the fingers which no-one else can see. My friend Barry Watts uses a shooing gesture, as if brushing away a fly, to accompany the command 'cancel, cancel, brush it [the negative thought] away'. Develop your own combination of thought and gesture and use them consciously for as long as it takes for them to become a habit.

Quickly replace any negative thought with a positive one. 'I can't think of anything' becomes 'I have all the ideas I need.' 'This is too hard' becomes 'In time all things are possible.' 'I'm not creative' becomes 'I *am* creative.' Since you cannot hold two thoughts at the same time, doesn't it make sense to hold the one which is most helpful to you?

If you doubt that this method works, fill in the rest of these phrases:

- I feel like a . . .
- When you're on a good thing . . .
- We're happy little . . .

If your mind didn't immediately supply the answers—Tooheys, stick to it, and Vegemites—you're either not Australian or don't own a television set. I've tried this in workshops and nearly everyone in the group can supply two out of three if not all three answers. Even if they don't use the products, the awareness is still there. Such is the power

32

of repeating messages over and over to our subconscious minds.

If it can work for beer and Vegemite, think what it can do for your idea factory.

In a nutshell

1   If you believe you aren't creative, or if you believe you are . . . you're right!
2   Send positive messages to yourself and others.
3   Change your beliefs to change the results. Try copying a picture upside down to teach yourself to see things in a new light.
4   Change your writing approach. Write your article as a poem, or a chapter of your novel in dialogue, to free yourself to get started.
5   Change your method of working—from a computer to a clipboard; from paper to a tape recorder.
6   Change your work location to free up your creativity.
7   Write your thoughts down instead of staring into space.
8   Practise seeing everyday events from several different points of view.

3

Right brain, right idea

Why must some writers struggle for every word while others seem to have more ideas than they can hope to write about?

According to William Manchester, the author of *American Caesar* and *Murdoch*, the fear of running dry is at the back of every writer's mind. The English novelist Keith Waterhouse says it can even lead to a reluctance to start work *in case* the ideas dry up. He tells the story of a writer who is starving in a garret when he is commissioned to do an article for a leading magazine. All he has to do is write a short piece on a subject he knows inside out and he'll pocket a substantial fee. The job has to be done by the end of August.

The deadline comes and goes and the writer hasn't delivered. He gets an extension until September, October, November . . . and still no article. Finally the editor sends an ultimatum. Is he going to write the article or not? Back comes the writer's response: 'Commencing article as soon as I have cleaned my tennis shoes.'

Being stricken with writer's block is more than being unable to write. Sometimes it's a kind of mental paralysis brought on by the very *idea* of writing, as this example illustrates.

Suddenly almost anything looks more attractive than writing—defrosting the refrigerator, de-fleaing the cat—it's amazing how creative a writer can be at avoiding the act of creation.

Right-brain perception

Bill Downey, in *Right Brain, Write On*, sees it as a problem of right-brain perception. Basically the brain has two hemispheres, the right brain and the left brain. A thick nerve cable called the corpus callosum allows communication and interaction between the two. While the brain has two distinct hemispheres, the terms 'right brain' and 'left brain' may encompass function as much as location, because an injury to one side of the brain does not always mean all functions attributed to that side are lost. It is probably more accurate to refer to the 'rational/systematic brain' and the 'creative brain' but the terms right and left brain are now so accepted that they will continue to be used here.

In right-handed people, the left brain deals with routine, explicit functions and directions. The right side generates

creativity and intuitive functions. The functions are reversed in left-handed people.

In most people the left side is dominant, controlling logical, rational thought. When you meet a new person, the left side responds to cues such as a firm handshake and warm smile. The intuitive right brain is the part cautioning you that something about this person 'isn't right'. Although we may discount this kind of input, it is frequently proven correct on longer acquaintance.

Christopher Columbus was a good example of resistance to left-brain injunctions. While he had sound reasons for believing that the world was round, the prevailing (left-brained) logic warned him that he would fall off the edge of the world. It must have taken all of his right-brained openness to new possibilities to override this logic and discover the New World.

Reading is a left-brain function. Writing is a right. Editing and keyboarding are left-brain. Generating ideas is right. The left side is generally more resistant to new and untried ideas. The right side is the part playing 'what if'.

Your natural idea factory

The right brain is your natural idea factory, but in a high-tech world, where survival can depend on dozens of minute-to-minute decisions from when to cross at the lights to how soon your credit card bill is due, it's no wonder that the left brain tries hard to remain in charge. In western society most people have a hard time quieting the left side of the brain in order to access their creative right side. The result is writer's block.

However, you *can* learn to access your right brain functions much more readily, once you understand the differences between the two and the conditions needed to make the switch.

Years ago, when I was involved in film scriptwriting, I found it almost impossible to type scripts in any sort of tidy format. Either the script looked great and sounded terrible, or it read well and looked like a dog's dinner.

Understanding the separate functions of right and left brain helped to solve this problem. If you've ever seen a film script, you'll recall that the format is specific and complicated. Scenes are numbered and described as internal or external, day or night. This information runs from the left to the right margin. Centred beneath this and across a slightly narrower measure are the 'stage' directions, actors' movements and scene description. Within narrower margins still is the dialogue itself. The name of the character speaking is centred above the dialogue.

Altogether, the writer has to cope with four different margin settings as well as keep track of hundreds of scene numbers. Setting out a script is about as left-brain a task as it's possible to imagine, even with the help of a computer. To make matters worse, some computers seem to take a fiendish delight in scrambling the format of a script when alterations are made.

Except for a fortunate few who can shift easily from one brain function to the other, most people have to work in one at a time. So trying to create a script—a right-brain activity—while setting it out in the required format—a left-brain function—is a recipe for disaster. You might as well try to play tennis with a golf club.

Creative solutions

Although I didn't know it at the time, my solution was creatively right-brained. I drafted the scripts on paper in longhand, paying only cursory attention to the format. Only after the script was written did I try to keyboard it into the accepted script format. This effectively separated the right- and left-brain functions so they were no longer in conflict.

Another writer friend took some accrued leave in order to write a long-dreamed-of novel. He rented a cottage by the ocean, provisioned it with everything he could possibly need and sat down at the computer to write, confidently expecting the words to flow.

They didn't.

Out of its familiar surroundings, his left brain remained stubbornly in charge, making it almost impossible for him to access his right-brain creativity. He only made progress by returning to his crowded city apartment and pounding out most of the novel while sitting at the kitchen table.

Again, it's easy to understand what happened. In familiar surroundings it was easier for the writer's logical, rational left brain to be quietened. There was less need for him to remain 'in control', and daydreaming became possible. In fact, ridding yourself of stress and worry is one of the best ways to get out of the left brain and into the creative right brain.

When you daydream, you're almost totally in right brain. Your critical faculties are suspended and you are seldom aware of time passing. Sometimes you have to go back and read your work to find out what you wrote. This is why 'write what you know' is such good advice. When your left brain is comfortable with the material you can drift into right-brain creativity more readily.

Creating the shift

In the Louvre in Paris, there's a particularly intriguing canvas. It is Rembrandt's *The Evangelist Matthew Inspired by the Angel* and shows a writer, pen in hand, expression thoughtful, as an angel whispers into his right ear. This is as vivid a depiction of the right brain at work as you are likely to find. If the angel represents right-brain creativity, the evangelist is certainly tuned in to his source of inspiration. So how can you persuade your own 'angels' to whisper into your ear?

The writer Edna Ferber preferred to work facing a blank wall or, failing that, a stretch of cloudless sky. Both of these engender a daydreaming mood in which you can forget yourself, as Anne Morrow Lindbergh put it. Driving along an open road invokes a mood of right-brain creativity for the essayist and novelist Joan Didion, and Agatha Christie recommended developing plots while doing the dishes.

All of these scenarios share a lack of disturbance or distraction. Doing mechanical tasks like the dishes lessens stress and enhances creative concentration. You can set yourself mundane tasks like tidying your desk or dealing with routine correspondence to settle your mind ready for the creative work ahead. Keeping a diary also helps you to shift into right brain, as it is a form of no-pressure writing.

The right brain will do almost anything to alleviate boredom. By deliberately setting yourself monotonous tasks such as retyping the last pages of your previous day's writing, or typing up columns from a newspaper, you can often trigger the flights of fantasy which signal a shift into right brain.

What if?

Writing the words 'what if?' at the top of a page and filling the page with outrageous possibilities is one of the best ways to shift into right brain.

It is important to suspend all criticism during this process. Make a deal with yourself to allow whatever comes, without editing or assessing it in any way. Asking myself, 'What if a romance heroine appeared nude in a centrefold?' gave me the idea for *Centrefold*. Asking 'What if a businesswoman hired a man as her "wife"?' led to *Man and Wife*, one of my most successful novels, which also tapped into a deep-rooted female fantasy. The results of the 'what if' process may surprise you, as the right brain is often more in touch with universal needs and wants than the critical left brain.

There are right- and left-brain versions of 'what if', however. 'What if my hero was a horse?' is right-brain and creative. 'What if I fail? What if they laugh at me?' is the voice of the left-brain critic which impedes creativity. Right-brain work is like crude oil. It must first be encouraged to flow before it can be refined.

Permission to create

Often, simply giving yourself permission to write any old how, even badly, can do the trick. Novelist Kate Grenville's maxim is 'It can all be fixed tomorrow.' This stops her getting too hung up on the task and enables her to be more creative.

Cultivating this awareness takes much of the anxiety out of writing, allowing you to slip into right brain much more readily, especially if you remind yourself that the object of the exercise is simply to tell a story. It's even simpler if you write non-fiction. Then your job is to explain a subject as clearly and enjoyably as possible.

Telling yourself this often enough will eventually quiet the left-brain critic sufficiently to allow your right-brain creativity to take over.

In writing workshops it's hard to free the right brain because of the pressure created by the group and time constraints. Giving everyone permission to write badly, acknowledging the difficulties, often helps.

It helps to use exercises for which there are no wrong answers. One such involves passing around envelopes containing slips of paper with adjectives and nouns on them. Participants take one of each and write about the resulting topic. Titles such as *Lonely Moon, Yellow Harvest, Velvet Rain* and *Distant Pearl* are some of the thought-provoking results.

Playing with words is a great way to access right-brain thinking. In 'Corn Corner', the Sydney *Sunday Telegraph* publishes the worst puns submitted by readers. Dreaming them up is a good right-brain exercise. Some of mine have included: What do you call books written by a clairvoyant? Seance fiction. How many letters are in the alphabet? 24, because ET went home. Puns may not be the highest form of wit, but they do force your brain into new (right-brain) patterns of thinking.

Try it for yourself. What does the word 'polyunsaturated' suggest? How about a waterproof parrot?

Nicknames are another form of wordplay with which you can experiment as an exercise in right-brain thinking. Pilot Light—always going out; Skyscraper—because of his tall stories; and Crime—doesn't pay, are examples. Try thinking of others.

Problem solving is a left-brain function and since the left is usually more dominant it tries to bulldoze its way through blocks, mostly without success. This is why writing problems frequently solve themselves when you give up and do something else like mow the lawn. Ridding yourself of stress and worry gets you out of left brain and into right.

There are other ways to help yourself make the shift. Ray Bradbury recommends writing every day to keep your writing 'muscles' flexible. When you do this, your left brain becomes more comfortable with the physical act of writing and your right can then concentrate on what you want to say.

Being thoroughly prepared for the task at hand also helps to reassure the critical left brain. But beware of over-preparation. Do only enough research to feel comfortable with the material. Tell yourself that extra details can be researched as the need arises. I use a printer's mark—t/c—which means 'to come'. If I can't think of the precise words to use, I put in more or less the right words, or a phrase which sums up the general direction of the thought, adding t/c in brackets afterwards. This saves interrupting the right-brain flow to search through dictionaries or reference books, which can be done at the (left-brain) editing stage later.

Dealing with interruptions

Think of right-brain creativity as a kind of bubble, fragile and easily burst. Interruptions are the pinpricks which are guaranteed to burst your creativity bubble, so it's important to keep them to a minimum.

Easier said than done? Probably, especially if you have to divide your attention between writing and the needs of a family. But it *can* be done.

Angela Devine has four children, a PhD in Classics, and has written many books. She tells her children that her writing may only be interrupted 'if there's blood or somebody is dead'. Even if you can only gain an hour a day by this method, writing just one page a day will give you a substantial manuscript by year's end.

Angela's rule works for her, and the children cope well with it, respecting their mother's work because she does. On one memorable day, however, one of the children knocked and timidly announced that another had apparently broken her leg. She was bouncing on the trampoline and the leg 'just broke', the child informed Angela. Jumping from the roof of a nearby shed may have had something to do with it.

Naturally these sorts of things make a parent feel hugely guilty for 'neglecting' the children, but such an accident can happen just as easily while you're washing dishes or ironing school uniforms. You need to remind your left brain of these facts, as guilt is a weapon much used by the left brain to stay in control. Remember, you may also have to convince *yourself* that you're working when you are staring out of a window.

Editing is a form of self-interruption, as it forces you to switch back and forth between right and left brain. If you're prone to editing your work after every few paragraphs, make a firm plan to do no more than glance at the previous output then keep writing. Avoid showing this raw output to others as an additional safety valve for your right brain.

Working in right brain is not a substitute for editing and polishing your work. It is a means of accessing your higher creative functions. The editing will come later out of left brain. Trying to do both at once is like trying to decorate a house while you're building it.

It's essential to establish your own best time for being creative, and this may involve some experimentation. Just as there are morning people and night people, there are morning and night writers. Very few work reliably from nine until five, although they may tell the media that they do.

From my experience, the reality is more like spending the first three hours shuffling objects around the desk or balancing the chequebook, followed by an hour or two of furious writing and another couple of hours of left-brain editing.

Only the two hours in the middle qualify as right-brain creative periods, but they are like the specks found when panning for gold. Nobody is surprised to find only a few specks of gold after sieving through huge piles of dirt. Therefore it shouldn't trouble a writer to spend several hours sifting through the left-brain dross for a couple of hours of right-brain gold.

Five steps to creativity

There are five steps you can take to help you get into right brain more quickly and reliably:

1 Establish a writing time which suits you and stick to it with as few exceptions as possible. If you don't take your writing seriously, no-one else will.
2 Establish a writing place, even if it's only a corner of a room. Going to this place at the same time each day establishes a mindset of being 'at work' which reassures your routine-loving left brain.
3 Have all writing materials near to hand before you start. Keep supplies and reference materials within easy reach. Working in unfamiliar surroundings and groping for tools is a sure way to keep yourself in left brain.
4 Give yourself permission to write anything, anyhow. Tell yourself it can all be fixed later. This silences the mental

critic which keeps you firmly in left brain. Also flatly refuse to edit *anything* you've written until it's substantially completed in draft.

5 Write what you know. This doesn't rule out fantasy or futuristic settings if you're comfortable with them. Do enough research beforehand to feel you're in familiar territory, then follow step 4 above.

Most importantly, tell the critic over your shoulder to shut up. Nobody has to see this anyway. It's only a rough draft to get your thoughts down on paper. Tell your critical left brain whatever you have to (lie if you must—it won't know the difference!) to free yourself sufficiently to get into that dreamy right-brain state in which your idea factory is in fullest flow.

Once you start working in right brain, resist the temptation to judge your work, for now anyway. The right brain has its own resources. Frequently my novels are interrupted by bits of business which pop into the first draft unannounced. That bit about my heroine having an adopted sister wasn't in the outline. But if the right brain says she should be there, who is the writer to argue? From experience I've learned that the sister will prove to be a pivotal character in a later chapter. Or an unusual hobby which a character unexpectedly develops will prove vital to the plot. Remember Grenville's Law: It can all be fixed tomorrow. If that stray fact thrown up by your right brain does prove to be a red herring, it can be removed at the editing stage.

You know you are working in right brain when time ceases to have meaning; when you have to go back and read through your work to find out what you wrote; when, as Anne Morrow Lindbergh says, 'pencils and pads and curling blue sheets alive with letters' heap up on the desk.

As Bill Downey observes, cultivating right-brain activity gives us 'a place to go, the place of our writing resources. The right brain will lead us there,' teaching us that it is 'okay to daydream, fantasise and wool-gather. Such is the stuff of creation.'

Find your dominant side

Is your left or right brain normally dominant? Ideally we should aim to become whole-brain thinkers, gaining the best benefits of both sides. Just as in sewing you need one hand to hold the fabric while the other manipulates the needle, you need both brain hemispheres to create and polish your writing. You could say that the right brain builds castles in the air while the left puts foundations under them. Just don't try to do both at the same time. Answer yes or no to the following questions to find whether your left or right brain generally dominates.

1 Do you like doing the same things at the same times each week?
2 Do you make quick assessments of the people you meet?
3 Do you enjoy playing games?
4 Do you believe in 'a place for everything and everything in its place'?
5 Do you carry an appointments diary and keep it up to date?
6 Have you tried a new activity in the last two weeks?
7 Is your motto 'one thing at a time'?
8 Do you enjoy the chance to do nothing?
9 Do you like puns and other forms of word play?

10 At restaurants do you choose foods you've never tried before?

11 Are you annoyed when your favourite TV program is replaced by another one?

12 A friend is going to Hawaii for the weekend and invites you along. Assuming there are no social or financial constraints, would you accept?

Analysis

1 Yes–2, No–1; 2 Yes–1, No–2; 3 Yes–1, No–2; 4 Yes–2, No–1; 5 Yes–2, No–1; 6 Yes–1, No–2; 7 Yes–2, No–1; 8 Yes–1, No–2; 9 Yes–1, No–2; 10 Yes–1, No–2; 11 Yes–2; No–1; 12 Yes–1, No–2.

18–24

You operate almost entirely out of left brain. To be more creative you need to learn to play, and become more comfortable with change and variety.

14–17

You are efficient and practical most of the time but can allow your creative right brain free rein at least half the time. Your only risk is that those 'Eureka moments' of true discovery may be restrained by your practical side.

14 or less

You work almost wholly out of right brain. Your problem is more likely to be keeping the wolf from the door as you pursue your creative interests. The da Vincis, Einsteins and Brett Whiteleys are likely to be in this group. Building castles in the air is easier for you than putting foundations under them.

In a nutshell

1   Your brain has two areas of activity known as the right brain and the left brain.
2   In most people the left brain deals with routine, explicit functions and directions. The right brain deals with creative and intuitive functions.
3   Your right brain is your natural idea factory, but in a high-tech society we need to learn to quiet the controlling left brain in order to become more intuitive and creative.
4   Working in familiar surroundings and doing mechanical tasks like filing and dishwashing makes it easier to shift into right brain.
5   Write 'what if' on a blank page and fill the page with outrageous possibilities straight from your right brain. Don't stop to edit them.
6   Give yourself permission to write, however badly, to take the anxiety out of the process.
7   Play with words and practise writing every day.
8   Write in right brain and edit in left. Don't try to do both at the same time.

4

Setting the scene

In order to have more and better ideas you need to convince yourself that it's okay to take risks. Ridicule and harsh criticism stifle creativity. Sharing your ideas with others can feel like undressing in public. There's ample potential for humiliation and ridicule. What if they laugh? What if they think my idea is stupid? What if my suggestion is not as good as the next person's?

This mental nagging comes under the heading of self-talk and this is where the 'thought switches' described in *Believing is Seeing* can help. It also helps to know that no-one is immune from nagging self-talk. Whether the self-talk is accurate or not—and usually it isn't—doesn't matter. What matters is its power to stop you from coming up with new ideas, far less sharing them with others.

Trust is half the battle

In *Drawing on the Right Side of the Brain* Betty Edwards says, 'You know more than you know you know'. This may sound like one of those sentences that don't make sense until punctuated properly, but think about it.

You know more than you know you know.

To put it another way, you know more than your unconscious mind usually admits to your conscious mind. Ideas that seem to spring fully formed from nowhere are usually synthesised from bits and pieces of information you weren't even aware of gathering.

When Gene Roddenberry, creator of the *Star Trek* universe, invented the character Mr Spock, he used a technique where he asked the character questions and wrote down the answers as they occurred to him. One question he wrote out for 'Mr Spock' (really Gene's own right brain) to answer was 'What is the universe for?'. The answer was 'The universe is a giant life and intelligence gathering mechanism.' This view turned out to be a cornerstone of many Eastern religions. Evidently, Gene's right brain had filed it away for future use. When needed, the information came to the surface as an idea.

The importance of mental work-outs

I happen to believe the mind is like a muscle. The more you use it, the more efficient it becomes. Giving your mind 'work-outs' in the form of word play such as making puns, playing Scrabble and other word games, and even looking up new words in the dictionary all help to strengthen your idea factory.

'Practising' being creative is no different from rehearsing a part in a play or preparing for a sporting event. Imagine running onto a playing field and expecting to play in the grand final with no preparation whatsoever. You might know all the rules of the game but your body would let you down. The same happens with mind work. Exercise your mind in as many ways as you can and it will be limber and ready when you want to start writing.

As a freelance advertising writer I shared offices with another writer who enjoyed puns as much as I did. One or other of us would make an excruciatingly bad pun on a subject. The other would then be expected to make one back on the same subject. Like verbal tennis players, we tossed puns back and forth as quickly as our minds could invent them, until the subject was exhausted.

Far from being a waste of time, this is the kind of limbering-up you can do to exercise your mental muscles. Just as exercise is fun with a serious purpose, so is word play.

Here's an example. Someone makes a comment about the weather and it's pun tennis time.

> No need to come *storming in* here to tell me that.
> I felt the mood needed *lightening* (lightning).
> You're right, I was feeling *under the weather*.
> Well I'll try to *rein* (rain) in my enthusiasm.
> Just so you don't go into *gales* of laughter.

Enough already. You get the idea. While games like this are more *sanuk* with a responsive partner, you can play them alone on paper. The aim is to see *whether* (weather) you can keep it up. Sorry.

Word games also quiet your critical left brain and subdue some of that self-talk which tries to tell you you aren't creative. It's the voice that's probably telling you right now that the very notion of making a chain of puns is silly, childish and time-wasting. It isn't. Like the exercises which warm up your body ready for sport, games like this warm up your mind for the very serious business of having ideas.

Remember, the more you tell yourself you are creative and practise creative activities, the more successful you will be at generating new ideas and getting them down on paper.

Conditions that foster creativity

In workshops I try to provide conditions that actively foster creativity. Making people feel *safe* is one of the most important elements. When they feel safe from ridicule or harsh criticism, my workshop participants are often surprised by the variety and originality of their ideas.

In *On Becoming a Person*, the psychotherapist Carl Rogers offered five conditions which he said one needs to fulfil in order to be creative. The first three are internal and the last two are external. They are:

- openness to new experiences
- the ability to make your own evaluations
- the ability to play
- psychological safety
- psychological freedom

Openness to new experiences

This means letting an experience happen at its own pace and in its own time, free of prior expectations and judgments. How many of us go to hear a speaker or turn on a TV program with our opinions already formed about the content? Sometimes all we hear are the things that confirm these opinions. Being open to the experience means really paying attention, not pre-judging or leaping to conclusions which may turn out to be wrong. It also means not arguing in your head if something unexpected, or with which you happen to disagree, is said.

The famous lateral thinker Edward de Bono coined the word 'po' to simply allow for possibilities. If you hear something new or strange, you can practise responding 'po' to yourself rather than the more judgmental 'yes' or 'no'. This leaves you open to whatever comes next.

You can also practise using 'po' when you find yourself at a talk or seminar which doesn't live up to your expectations. Instead of grumbling to yourself about the waste of time and money, you can recoup some of your investment by paying attention only to the speaker's message if it's the style that bothers you. Or resolve to learn from the presentation what *not* to do when speaking in public. This way you turn a potentially negative experience into a positive learning experience.

The ability to make your own evaluations

Having said 'po' to a possibility, you can then mull it over, consider all the factors and reach your own conclusion. This ability quiets the self-talk which is invariably critical and hampers a creative mind-set.

Making your own evaluations is more creative because it reduces your dependence on others' opinions of you. Only you can decide whether you're creative. If a parent or parental figure once accused you of lacking originality, you can reserve judgment until all the facts are in. Remember they didn't have all the facts either, and probably based this judgment of you on limited examples of your behaviour. Don't make the same mistake when evaluating yourself.

The ability to play

In an old episode of *Star Trek*, Captain Kirk says 'The more complex the mind, the greater the need for the simplicity of play.' This is an important condition for fostering creativity because play is primarily a right-brain activity. Modern technology is not fulfilling our need for play, according to the child psychologist Dr John Irvine. He says technology such as VCRs, computers and television 'package the creative factor' without demanding the use of imagination, practical problem-solving, conflict resolution and negotiation.

We all need to play, he says, for relaxation and to avoid stress-related disorders. Play is a natural anti-stress exercise which helps to release endorphins and other natural chemicals which make us feel good.

According to Dr Irvine, two of the most important ingredients for successful (creative) play are an absence of strict time limits and an atmosphere of safety and security.

People who can't play are likely to have furniture which has 'put down roots'. They buy products and wouldn't dream of altering them to suit themselves. How it came is how it is 'meant' to be, they argue. Meant by whom?

Playing with your environment fosters creativity as surely as does playing with words and ideas. So make up your mind to rearrange your furniture occasionally. Try wearing your clothes in different combinations, rather than in their original pairings. Try a new hairstyle or colour. All of these activities will help you to become more playful and comfortable with change and novelty.

Writing teacher Barry Watts suggests breaking old habits by 'catching yourself thinking'. He advises switching hands when you soap yourself in the shower each day. Even such a small change in your routine helps to shake up your thinking.

You'll be surprised how resistant you are to doing things differently, and how strong will be the urge to switch the soap back to the 'correct' hand.

Another exercise in playful thinking is to cross your arms and note which arm is uppermost. Now cross them again with the other arm on top. When we do this in workshops the usual result is a tangle of arms and much laughter, because the habit of putting the same arm on top each time is so strong—yet we're barely aware of doing it.

According to Carl Rogers there are also two internal conditions you need to satisfy to foster creativity:

Psychological safety

This means having people around you who aren't going to make it hard for you to try something new.

Mention any new idea in a group and watch how quickly you are told why it won't work, or why you can't do whatever it is. Or that it's been tried before without success. In the following chapters you'll discover some useful strategies for dealing with these critics, or with your internal critic. For now you can simply tell the 'no' person that it disturbs you when they prejudge your idea before you've had the chance to explore it fully.

If the other person persists with their negative comments it may be wise to keep your ideas to yourself until you have developed them more fully. You can also actively seek out people who *will* support your attempts to be more adventurous in your thinking. In *Think and Grow Rich*, Napoleon Hill calls these your Mastermind group. They can be friends, family, a writers' workshop group or any group of like-minded people who are committed to supporting each others' ideas. Naturally you will want to work on responding positively to the ideas of others so *you* aren't the 'no' person in a group.

Psychological freedom

Someone once said that when you have a new idea you're in a minority of one. It's human nature to want to fit in, to be liked and accepted by our peers. Society also says we should always know what we're doing and where we're going. Yet creativity is a voyage of exploration—and sometimes a mine-field.

To be truly creative you need the freedom *not* to know where you're going with an idea. You need to be able to think and feel whatever you think and feel without having to justify yourself or meet the expectations of others. This freedom can frighten some people, both those trying to escape the mould and those dealing with the escapees. Any time you doubt this, try pouring honey over your potatoes at a dinner party, or eating your ice-cream with a knife.

You can provide your own climate of psychological freedom by allowing yourself to do such things, and any others which take your fancy, alone and in private if necessary, until you feel comfortable with breaking petty 'rules'. As long as no-one else gets hurt by your actions the world won't come to an end because you eat your peas with honey. As a piece of doggerel says, 'It makes the peas taste funny but it keeps them on my knife.'

Here are some other examples of rule-breaking behaviour. Try them or make up your own.

- Drink coffee out of a cereal bowl.
- Eat cereal out of a coffee mug.
- Shower in your underwear. If nothing else, it's a great time-saver.
- Write an article as a poem, a poem as a letter, a short story as a memo. Tom Wolfe, totally blocked on a subject,

wrote an article as a memo to his editor. The editor ran
the memo and Wolfe wrote all his articles as memos from
then on.

- Buy a roll of cheap fax paper. Write on the roll, letting
the uncut paper spill over the edge of your desk as you
write until you have metres of it. (Don't submit it to an
editor like this, or if you do, don't tell them it was my
idea.)
- Lie flat on your back and stare at the sky or ceiling. Write
about what you see projected there. In a *Peanuts* cartoon,
Linus and Charlie Brown were staring at the clouds. Linus
visualised famous people and great events. Charlie Brown
said he was going to say he saw a doggie and a horse,
but thought he'd better not. Moral: If you stare at ceiling
or clouds, keep your visions to yourself to foster a climate
of psychological safety. Leonardo da Vinci recommended

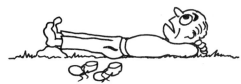

See visions in clouds !

staring at a wall spotted with stains to discover 'an endless variety of objects' to arouse the mind 'to various inventions'.

When the five conditions are met, you will be much more open to the special moments known as inspiration. They are not always easy to achieve but they *can* be achieved if the climate is right.

Too often we restrict ourselves with musts, shoulds and oughts which are not rules so much as they are excuses. A favourite film which emphasises this is *Drop-Out Father*. It stars Dick Van Dyke as a harassed father of three unappreciative teenagers. His main function seems to be to support their credit card habits and a heavily mortgaged house. One day at work a colleague drops dead, prompting Van Dyke's character to reevaluate his priorities.

Over protests that he has ruined his family's life, he sells the house, cuts up all the credit cards and moves to a loft apartment to become a freelance photographer. This is Hollywood, so everyone lives happily ever after, but the story does serve to illustrate how few restrictions we really have in life.

Many of the trappings of modern life which are supposedly indispensable are, in reality, choices which keep us bound to a certain course in order to pay for them. In effect we mortgage our souls. 'Keeping up with the Joneses' has been rephrased as 'improving our standard of living'. But is it really an improvement if it gets in the way of achieving your full creative potential?

You can't be creative if you are at odds with yourself; if you're an accountant who would rather be writing thrillers, say. The most creative people are those who are doing what they enjoy most, either in their working lives or, at the very least, in their free time.

Creativity work-out

Five steps you can take to develop your creativity:

1 *Challenge yourself to find more and better ideas*
   Believe it or not, some writers become so wedded to one idea that they build an entire career around it. This is fine if the project is something as spectacular as Steven Spielberg's *E.T. The Extra-Terrestrial* or Tom Keneally's *Schindler's Ark*—although these people would be the last to devote their careers to one idea. But with some writers, it's as if they fear they will never get another idea as good. They lovingly polish and develop this one idea until all the juice runs out of it and it's as lifeless and dehydrated as an old prune.

   A copywriter with whom I worked in advertising had written *one* romance novel in her teens and still talks of editing it for submission to a publisher. The lady is 74. Can you imagine how current this book would be now? Another writer wrote a children's book based on Aboriginal mythology. A publisher showed some interest but nothing came of it. Two decades later the writer is still clinging to the project, although it has almost no hope of acceptance in the present-day ideological climate.

2 *Don't fall so in love with an idea that you become wedded to it*
   Imagine you have a client who requires one new project idea every week. It must be on her desk by noon every

Friday without fail. Whether you seek to develop ideas for poetry, short stories or books, this is a guaranteed way to force yourself to produce new ideas.

This method works, as I learned when I worked in advertising. Deadlines were the bane of my existence. They were always too early, yet I can't recall ever missing one. Often the work was ready ahead of deadline, although I never told the client it was. He might think it came too easily and want to pay me less for it.

It's one of the crazy realities of advertising that clients will pay you for almost anything *but* the idea, although without an idea you have nothing to sell. I often wrote out invoices for copywriting, consulting work, provision of materials, travelling time and expenses—just about everything except thinking. Yet the thinking was what produced the value. Everything else was hack work.

Set deadlines for yourself and stick to them. You'll be amazed how it increases your productivity and the number of new ideas you're able to generate.

3   *Play with your ideas*
What you've developed so far are the bare bones of ideas for future writing projects. Now it's time to explore all the possibilities they contain.

Don't be too quick to pin down an idea with specifics. You may be able to combine several ideas to make a really dynamite short story or novel premise. In my experience, the biggest mistake many writers make is to go off half-cocked with an idea which has just burned itself through their brain. They are so impatient to start writing that they fail to explore all the angles. They should first ask themselves 'What else?', 'What next?' and 'What more can I do to make this special?'

In workshops I talk about *layering* a plot. By this I mean starting with a basic idea and fleshing it out with still more developments and complications. Just as a sandwich would be fairly unexciting if all you put between the slices of bread was a thin slice of ham, a story is very unsatisfying if all you have is one meagre idea. Like sandwiches, stories need plenty of meat.

They also benefit from seasoning in the form of plot complications, and garnishing in the form of richly developed characters.

Nurture your ideas. Play with them. Give them a chance to grow to full maturity before you rush to start writing.

4   *Make your idea earn its keep*
Practically everyone advises you to write down your ideas and file them so you don't forget them. This is sound

advice and good practice for your writing muscles. One writer I read about has a set of files marked 'interesting stuff' and 'even more interesting stuff'.

So why don't more of these ideas blossom into stories and books? I keep an idea file, but I can't remember the last time I pulled something out of the file and built a story around it. Why not?

My friend Des Theodore recommends being honest with yourself. 'When you have an idea you shouldn't say, "What a clever boy (or girl) I am." Ask yourself: "Did the earth *really* move?" ' For some people, having any idea at all does seem like a miracle, he says, quoting the people who, as soon as they know you're a writer, say, 'I've had an idea for a book. You write it and we'll go halves on the profits.'

These drawersful of scribbled notes are more likely to be a repository of ordinary ideas, says Theodore. The scribbles themselves mean nothing. You could be like Lawrence Block and subscribe to an idea service if one existed, and you'd acquire a drawerful pronto. By whatever means you accumulate them, that's what they are—scribbles. They could just as well be pages from the phone book, newspaper articles, old love letters or publishers' rejection letters. When you go through these notes, see one of the scribbles and say 'Wow!'—*that's* when you have a good idea, according to Theodore.

The other side of the coin is the idea that is so strong it tugs at you, bugs you and won't go away. Usually an idea this strong will compel you to build a structure around it, such as a few hundred words of narrative, dialogue or a description of how the idea would work. This kind of idea is the most worthy of your attention, but even it must be made to earn its keep. Play with the idea for a long time, both on paper and in your mind. Examine it from every angle. Jot down thoughts and random notes about it as they occur to you, but don't attempt to organise them into anything coherent just yet.

This kind of idea should be like the chemicals you squirt out of a spray can to fill a hole in a wall. When they hit the hole they expand to fill all the available space and only then do they set rigid, needing to be sanded to tidy them up.

5   *Train yourself to sort the wheat from the chaff*
Writing down your ideas and putting them into a file is a good way to unclutter your mind. I find that if I don't write an idea down it nags at me and keeps me awake (since ideas invariably strike me at night). Writing down these fleeting notions gives me peace of mind and freedom to concentrate on other projects.

Every so often, go through the idea file and test your reactions, says Theodore. If one of your snippets sends your thoughts soaring or gives you goose bumps, pull it out for further development. The ones you look at and wonder, 'Why did I think that was so great?' are the ones you can safely discard. They've passed their use-by date.

Des Theodore calls these 'junk ideas', likening them to junk mail. Just as with junk mail there's an occasional grain of enlightenment among the dross, so too will your idea file occasionally yield such gems.

To further train yourself to spot good ideas, study the world around you. Look at what appeals to you and what appeals to masses of other people. Concentrate on the things that appeal to both you and many others. If you like a

63

particular pop star or classical performer, ask yourself, out of all their recordings which produces the biggest emotional reaction? Is it their best-selling recording? Why? How does it manage to affect you and so many others wherever and whenever it is played? At some concerts the opening bars of a particular song are enough to spark an immediate reaction from the audience.

Don't just say it's a great piece of music or a terrific song. Ask yourself why. What is there about it that appeals to so many people, including yourself? Be as specific as you can about the source of the appeal.

Now do the same with paintings, cartoons, buildings, bridges, ancient monuments, furniture designs, fashions, cars, landscapes both man-made and natural, including sunsets, starry nights and snow-covered mountains.

This exercise will help you tune in to whatever moves great numbers of people, including you. You'll better understand why some ideas move people so strongly and why others, apparently every bit as sound, leave them—and you—cold.

It's a five-finger exercise for writers.

Learn to relax

This may seem to contradict Step 1 above, which involves setting deadlines and forcing yourself to have more ideas, but it actually complements it.

Learning to relax gives your creative right brain time to play with an idea uninterrupted by your more critical left brain. Lack of action frustrates and bores your right brain, and this is a good thing. The more you delay acting on an idea, the more frenzied your right brain is likely to become, throwing up new possibilities and combinations until you are virtually forced to take notice.

During this stage, get as far away from the writing process as you can. If you write for a living, do some other work. If you are hatching a fiction idea, develop a non-fiction article, for instance. Write letters. But don't talk about the idea simmering on the back burner of your mind. Ernest Hemingway believed that talking about an idea squeezed the 'juice' out of it. He may have been right. Your right brain revels in the new and different. Talking about an idea may well satisfy your right brain's need to develop the project. It doesn't much care whether you write the idea out or talk it out. Either way it is old news once you've given the idea an airing, and your right brain won't want anything more to do with it. So save your 'juice' for the actual writing.

Learn a relaxation exercise that works for you. Just as physical exercise tones your body, relaxation tones your mind, making it more receptive to ideas and more disciplined in handling them.

For the past three years I've practised chakra meditation, which involves focusing on the seven major energy centres of the body. If you're interested in learning more about chakra meditation as it applies to writing, you can contact the Pegasus Education Group at PO Box 1, Springvale Victoria 3171, for books and tapes. The tape I use features hypnotherapist Barry Konicov, and is produced by Potential Unlimited and distributed by Transworld Publishers Australia.

While you relax, visualise yourself as having already accomplished your writing goal. See the book, story or article as a finished product. Picture your name on it. Visualisation is important enough to require a chapter of its own, but for now be aware that you need to picture the project as already existing in all its glory.

During relaxation periods, take time out to enjoy your world. Go for a walk and closely observe everything around you. Soak up the details, the sights, sounds, smells and subliminal messages your senses are receiving. This activity also helps to quiet your critical left brain and gives you more access to the creative right brain.

Sit down and write

I can almost hear you thinking, 'It's easy for you to say.' This is possibly the hardest step to accomplish and the one which writers, myself included, become masters at putting off. The scriptwriter William Goldman calls it 'putting off doomsday'.

There is only one sure-fire antidote to putting off doomsday—stop doing it. Put a sheet of paper in the typewriter or boot up the computer—and start. Write foolish, idiotic, nonsensical things. If you can, steer the nonsense along the general lines of your project. But start. As Goethe said, 'Beginning has power and magic in it.'

If it helps, give yourself permission to start in the middle or at the end. It was only your school English teachers who insisted you start at the beginning, and they're probably long gone from your life. Who knows, from what I hear about the current process-orientated approach to the teaching of writing, they may not tell you to start at the beginning any more. If so it's definitely progress.

Write something, anything, but write. Don't stop to fetch that cup of coffee you suddenly remember you need. Don't go to the bathroom. Or look at just one more piece of research. These urges come from your left brain, which is trying to stay in charge. Refuse to let it. This is right-brain time. Or should that be 'write brain'?

In a nutshell

1   The mind is like a muscle. Give it mental work-outs by playing with words, games and using the dictionary.
2   To foster your creativity, aim to: be open to new experiences; make your own evaluations; be able to play; and give yourself psychological freedom and a safe atmosphere in which to take risks.
3   To develop your creativity, follow five steps:
    — find more and better ideas
    — tell yourself there will always be another idea
    — play with your ideas before becoming specific
    — keep an idea file but make every entry earn its keep
    — train yourself to recognise the good ideas from the 'junk ideas'.
4   Try to pin down what attracts large numbers of people to certain music, paintings, books etc.
5   Learn a relaxation technique to free up your right brain.
6   Stop 'putting off doomsday'—sit down and write.

5

Start seeing UFOS

Being creative is an active state, not a passive one. To be creative you need to create *something*. Previously we looked at the five conditions you need to fulfil in order to be able to create. As you've seen, you can meet these conditions for yourself. Now you are ready for the next stage, which is to actively cultivate the kind of original thinking that will make what you write stand out from the crowd.

For easy memorising, I've labelled the four skills you require UFOS. They don't come from outer space, although maybe that point is moot, too, since no-one really knows where ideas come from. Personally I think they come from an ability to make new combinations out of existing thoughts and elements. Asked what is 2 + 2, a creative person might say '22', which you get when the figures are placed side by side. But they could also say 'A pair of swans', which is what the figures resemble.

Test yourself. Look at this list and pick the odd one out:

duck
drake
dog
dodo
emu

If you said 'dog' you're correct, as it is the only member of the group which is not a bird. It is also the only four-legged creature on the list. However if you said 'emu' you'd also be right. It's the only word which doesn't start with the letter 'd'. But 'dodo' might also be right, as it is the only member of the group which is extinct. And 'drake' is the only word on the list with more than four letters. So there are at least four 'correct' answers to the question. All are equally valid depending on how you choose to look at it. Remember, the hallmark of creativity is being able to 'see in a new way'.

So maybe seeing UFOS isn't a bad way to approach the whole question. The people who report seeing them are certainly open to new experiences and able to make their own evaluations and play (with the idea of extra-terrestrials visiting Earth). In order to share their experiences they need an atmosphere of psychological freedom and psychological safety, so all five conditions are met.

You can see UFOS at any time of the day or night, any time in fact when you need to push your thinking beyond the usual boundaries. UFOS stands for:

Unlimited
Flexible
Original
Specific.

Unlimited

To get yourself out of the critical left brain and into the creative right brain you need to remove some of the barriers between the two. Take away the limits. For this you need a large number of ideas, the larger the better.

For example, how many uses can you think of for a plastic ice-cream container? Before you read on, take a moment to make a list. Be as bizarre and adventurous as you can without restricting yourself in any way. The aim is to make your list as long as possible.

In workshops the list has included: children's stilts (with string handles threaded through the sides and the containers turned upside down); shelf; planter; mouse house; toy boat; fake rock for the garden (when covered with papier mâché and painted); base for a statue; mouse trap; serving dish or plate (with the sides cut down); diskette or recipe file; helmet to ward off marauding magpies; Hannibal the Cannibal mask (as worn in the film *Silence of the Lambs*, with cut-outs for mouth and eyes); lamp shade; seedling protector (with the base removed); bush shower (holes punched in the base); hanging basket for plants; mud-brick mould; and dozens of other possibilities. How long was your list?

It helps to decide to list a minimum number of uses before you let yourself stop. If you aim to think of 20 uses for an ice-cream container, the first half-dozen will be the ones everyone thinks of. The next ten will be a little more original because you'll be forced to think harder. But it's the last two or three that will contain the real gold of original thinking, because by then you will feel desperate enough to write down just about anything.

This method came in handy when I needed to think of a new title for a romance novel. I'd already discussed several alternatives with my editor and settled on *A Bride for a Prince*, which seemed to have just the right aura of romance plus the curiosity value of the royal connection.

Unfortunately, at the same time I was asked to rename a book called *Truth to Tell*. The publishers know that books with a wedding connection in the title usually sell well, so I called this book *Sister of the Bride*. Having two 'bride' titles close together could become confusing, so this meant changing the title of the first book.

Since I had discarded half a dozen alternatives before deciding on *A Bride for a Prince*, the most obvious titles were already accounted for. I set myself the task of coming up with 25 titles (a purely arbitrary figure). Eventually I arrived at *A Royal Romance*, the title under which the book was finally published.

This may seem like a lot of work to come up with an apparently simple title, but the purpose of a title isn't to show off the author's cleverness. The idea is to flag to readers to the contents of the book and interest them sufficiently so they pick the book out from among dozens of titles.

Sometimes the simplest ideas are the hardest to pin down. I have a lot of sympathy for the copywriter who came up with 'Coke adds life', as I can imagine the hours and hours of thinking and the many hundreds of alternatives that would have been considered and discarded before arriving at that simple but memorable phrase.

In *The Trouble with Tribbles*, the science fiction writer David Gerrold recounts a similar experience while scripting an episode of the same name for *Star Trek*. Tribbles are little furry creatures which breed so rapidly they threaten to take over. In his early drafts Gerrold called the creatures Fuzzies, mainly so he could call the script *A Fuzzy Thing Happened*. Then he discovered a science fiction novel called *Little Fuzzy* by H. Beam Piper. Its premise was entirely different but using the same name posed a slight legal risk, so Gerrold decided it was wiser to rename his creatures.

His list, reproduced in his book, included: shagbies, shaggies, shappies, gollawogs, callahans, callies, goonies, goomies, goombahs, combahs, roonies, charlies, trippies, tribbles, triblets, trippets, willies, brazzies, triffles, piffles, puffies, poofies 'and a whole lot of other silly words'.

You can see how far down the list the writer was before he came to 'tribbles', which the creatures eventually became. Incidentally, this became one of the series' most memorable and best-loved episodes and the tribbles themselves became a toy phenomenon. Who knows whether they would have enjoyed the same success had not David Gerrold forced himself to be unlimited in his thinking.

Flexible

As well as being unlimited, your thinking also needs to be flexible. This is the kind of mind-set which allows you to see

'2 + 2' as 22 or a pair of swans. Don't just look at things as they are or have always been, but as they *might* be.

For example when I needed a pair of small shelves to support two compact stereo speakers, I couldn't find anything in the shops small enough to do the job. I could have bought larger shelves and cut them down to size or had some made to my requirements, but I did neither of these things. In the interest of being flexible, I decided to stop looking for 'shelves' and look for 'things which could hold up speakers'.

Since I was no longer shopping specifically for shelves I could get out of the shelving department and look anywhere in the store where I might find things to hold up speakers.

Try it! Suddenly I had the entire department store at my disposal, including such unlikely places as the toy department and the bathroom fittings section. Guess what? That's where I finally found my 'speaker shelves'. They were a pair of flat

OK, who's got the soapholder?

tortoiseshell acrylic soap dishes, very modern in design, with gold fittings. Better still, they were exactly the size and shape I needed and could be screwed to the sides of my entertainment unit in minutes. They even came complete with screws. Without the flexibility to think beyond shelves, I might never have solved the problem so satisfactorily—or so inexpensively.

A creative mind is flexible. It doesn't pay to become hidebound in your thinking or to assume that anything can only be done one way, especially if you're confronted with pat phrases like 'We've always done it that way.' We live in the era of what Alvin Toffler has called future shock, and change is part of our daily lives. Like the dinosaurs, if we don't adapt we will perish.

Being able to see things from more than one point of view is helpful when it comes to editing your work. This is a task which really bothers some writers and I think computers have a lot to answer for in this regard. They make even your rough drafts look like finished work, which can be daunting. Who wants to mess up a pristine-looking page with revisions?

When I sat down to write this book I decided to do it as much in right brain as possible, so I ended up writing the first draft on a typewriter. I tried keyboarding it into my electronic word processing machine's memory but found that inhibiting, as my left brain stayed in charge. As with the scriptwriting, I could either do a messy draft which read well or a neat draft which lacked all passion and fire.

So sometimes it pays to be messy with your first drafts. One writer says he prints his drafts on the backs of old correspondence so he isn't tempted to submit them to a publisher. Using coloured paper is another way of reminding yourself that this is draft copy, subject to change and improvement. All these approaches help you to work in right brain initially.

Another tip to keep you flexible while editing is to ask yourself what *work* this piece of writing has to do. It's my favourite question at every stage of the writing process. If you know what purpose each paragraph, page or chapter is to serve and you apply the requirement of flexibility, you can write or rewrite the piece in any number of ways to achieve that goal.

For example, in a recent novel of mine there was a scene in which the heroine's niece, upset by the news of her parents' impending divorce, goes out onto a high window ledge to think things over. The hero 'talks' her down. My editor, concerned that the suicide implication might be too gritty for a fantasy medium, suggested a change. But to what? The idea of having the hero talk the teenager down while the heroine watched from the ground had a lot of appeal. How much more heroic could he get?

There lay the answer. By following the rules of staying flexible and focusing on the work the scene had to do, I was able to come up with a scene which did the job even better than the 'suicide' one.

Stripping away the trappings of the scene, I decided its purpose was to put the hero in real jeopardy and allow the heroine to realise how important he had become to her. Any scene which placed the hero in danger for the heroine to witness would do the same job. Suddenly the options were many and various.

The published scene has the niece heading for her school's music room, where she likes to go to think things over. Following her, the hero and heroine see her crossing the street just as a juggernaut of a truck comes roaring around a corner.

The hero races forward and pushes the teenager out of the way, but is clipped by the truck and dislocates his shoulder. His bravery and dismissal of his injury allow the heroine her moment of realisation, and the stage is set for a happy ending.

When you are faced with an editing problem, go back and ask yourself what work the piece of writing was intended to do. Was it meant to reveal character? Move the story forward? Push the characters into some new discovery? Create a particular mood? If the answer is none of the above, consider editing the scene out altogether. Nobody said it would be easy.

But being flexible makes it easier.

Original

After you've opened yourself to all the possible ideas and angles on a writing question, it's time to start eliminating and combining ideas. Out of all the possible alternatives, you have to ask yourself, which is the most original solution to the problem?

For example, in the scene described above, I could probably have had the niece go missing and let the hero and heroine spend some anxious moments waiting for news of her. Or looking for her. The trouble is, this has been done dozens of times. Maybe having the hero push the teenager out of the path of a truck isn't the single most original solution in the world, but it's a big improvement on the lost-child scenario. As an exercise, see if you can improve on my solution. If so, let me know. Better still, write your own version and make a fortune.

Original feels good

How will you know when you've come up with an original idea? For a start, it will *feel* good. You'll get goose bumps and the hair will rise on the back of your neck. Trust me, ideas are like that. They grab you and through you they grab other people as well. But they have to excite you first.

It's like the question every teenager asks—how will I know when I'm in love? Every adult's answer is the same—you'll just know. And you'll know when you're staring at an idea that's sufficiently special to be worth pursuing at the expense of all the alternatives.

The trick is not to go with the first or even the most promising idea you think of until you've filled an arbitrary quota of alternatives. You may be staring at a great idea, but there may be an even better one further down the list. If you don't stick with it you may never know what you've missed.

Specific

This is the last step in the UFOS formula. Strangely enough, it's the one most writers want to rush ahead with as soon as possible because it feels like action. It feels like you're making progress. But if you start on this step too soon you may well be making progress in the wrong direction.

One of my clients used to be famous for his impatience. A real high flier, he was always anxious to get things moving and hated any kind of painstaking preparation. 'Let's move on it' was his favourite phrase. One day he was running late for a speaking engagement and jumped into a passing taxi. 'Move on it,' he instructed the bewildered driver. 'Let's go, let's go, we're wasting time.' They had been driving for some distance at a speed which bore little resemblance to the limit when the executive asked, 'Where are we going?' 'I don't know, sir,' said the driver, 'but we're making fantastic time.'

Make sure you don't start getting specific with your idea until you've made an exhaustive list of all your options. In the scene from my novel I set out to list 20 ways in which I could put the teenager in jeopardy so my hero could rescue her. They ranged from shooting incidents to train wrecks, a fainting spell on the girl's part, a bag-snatching. I really put the poor girl through hell before deciding to throw her under the wheels of that truck.

When it was time to get specific, I eliminated options one at a time by imagining them as I would write them. The bag-snatching seemed promising but, like the teenage suicide threat, was a little too close to reality for an escapist novel. It might have worked well in a suspense thriller. The fainting spell was unexciting, the train wreck was impractical, and most of the other possible solutions didn't flow naturally from the scenes that went before.

As you can see, this is a process of elimination. Just don't start eliminating until you're sure you've pushed yourself to the limit thinking up every possible alternative. Only then jump into the passing cab, because by then you'll know precisely where you're going.

Use UFOS in business writing, too

This method works equally well when it comes to business writing. If you have to write a memo to your employees, first ask yourself what result you want it to achieve.

Say you decide you have to get your employees to work on time. You can focus on how this might be achieved. Start by asking yourself why it's important to have everybody there on time. Will your customers be disadvantaged if there aren't enough people to look after them? Are you being picky? Or are you really annoyed because you're the only person turning up on time and you're jealous of the others' freedom? Maybe the others stay at work later or work through their breaks.

Once you focus on the result you want the memo to achieve and you know why it is important, you will be able to phrase the memo in the best way to get the results you want.

Using the UFOS approach, first look for alternatives. Focus on *content* rather than on method and you'll discover you have far more options than you ever suspected.

In a nutshell

1 Be unlimited. Set a minimum number of ideas and don't stop until you've listed that number. Be as bizarre and adventurous as you can.
2 Be flexible. Look at your options as they *might* be rather than as they are or have always been.
3 Identify the *work* the piece of writing has to do. This lets you explore the many ways it can be achieved.
4 Be original. After listing all the possibilities, start to combine and eliminate ideas until you find the most exciting one. You'll recognise an original idea because it *feels* good.
5 Be specific. Eliminate options until you find the one that works best and is most original within the demands of your project.
6 Use the UFOS method in business writing. First focus on the result you want to achieve and why you want to achieve it, then follow steps 1 to 5 above.

6

Pulling out the stops

Writers are very good at what William Goldman calls 'putting off doomsday'. As with the writer who couldn't get started until he'd cleaned his tennis shoes, there are more excuses per square writer than there are reasons to actually start working. Do you recognise any or all of these?

I'll write when:

I have time.
I get a better typewriter/computer/laptop.
I get my chair fixed.
I have a really good idea.
The weather is warmer/cooler.
I'm not so exhausted.
The kids go back to school.
Christmas/New Year/Easter is over.
I get over this cold/flu that's going around.
I finish my research.
I've defrosted the refrigerator.
I've clipped my toenails.
My house guests leave.
My children grow up.
The world becomes perfect.

If you'd rather play this game than write, by all means go ahead and list all the ones I've missed. You'll find they are mostly variations on the above anyway.

For my money, every one of these excuses is precisely that, an excuse. *Nobody* ever has all the time, money, conditions and ideas they want before they start writing. If we wait until we do, the world will have turned into a ball of ice and humans will be long gone from its surface.

I'll say it again. *Nobody* ever has the ideal writing conditions. Some of the most successful books, plays, short stories and poems were written under the most difficult conditions. Sometimes lack of money is the spur to doing in a shorter time span what would otherwise take the writer many months.

Create your own deadlines

There's a law that says 'work expands to fill the time available'. Housework ditto. Creative writing especially ditto. As one who's had published some 35 novels, 16 non-fiction books, a multi-volume children's science encyclopaedia, two novellas, a couple of short stories, about 20,000 words of a gardening encyclopaedia, 150 newspaper columns, maybe three dozen articles on various subjects, two feature film scripts, two documentary film scripts and a score or more of miscellaneous writing projects (not counting my previous life as an advertising writer), I can guarantee that the longer you have to complete a project, the more time it will take. Trust me on this.

Romance publishers Harlequin Mills & Boon generally don't set deadlines for their writers. They say they'd rather have a better quality manuscript which takes a little longer than a so-so one produced to a deadline. They could be right, I don't know. Their North American stablemates Silhouette Books *do* set deadlines and the quality of their books is frequently excellent. So both approaches work.

For books without deadlines, I set my own. They become as inviolate as any set by a publisher. Maybe I even take them a bit more seriously, because it's too easy to get lax and unproductive otherwise.

Two hints about setting your own deadlines: set them just beyond your personal 'comfort zone' so you'll work just a little bit harder; and tell everyone else that you'll need a month longer than you're sure you will need. This means you have some extra time up your sleeve to deal with problems as they arise without letting anyone else down. Do not include that month's grace in your *own* deadline, not even mentally. For you it doesn't exist. Giving others your real deadline gives you no scope to be appreciated as a miracle worker. Hence the double deadline: a private one for yourself and a contractual one for other people.

If you do sign a contract with a deadline, assuming there is a little leeway, try to put your 'extra' month in writing. It's better for your self-esteem to supply the manuscript early than to have to explain why it's late. But no matter what your contract says, set your own personal deadline a month earlier than the agreement requires.

This is a private challenge which is virtually guaranteed to spur you on to greater achievement. With practice you'll become skilled at estimating and setting your own deadlines and they will become as pressing to you as those in any contract, which is as it should be.

The only two excuses

No matter how many excuses you've included in your 'why I can't write' list, for me there are only two that matter. Conquer them and the others will vanish along with them. The two reasons why most writers don't write as much as they would like to are:

- fear of failure
- lack of real interest

I'll address the second reason first because it may save you reading any further if you find it applies to you.

Some people find that *being* a writer is the most important part of things. They enjoy going to conferences, attending workshops, doing courses and entering competitions. In the romance field there are many competitions which require entrants to submit a synopsis and sample chapters of a book. I know one Australian writer who has entered and won several of these competitions yet never had a book accepted for publication, or even finished writing one, to my knowledge. Her specialty is writing partials, outlines and sample chapters. She knows how to hook a reader, get the characters together quickly and make the sparks of conflict really fly. She writes wonderful two-page outlines. But she's scared stiff of writing an entire book because she's never tackled one yet.

Maybe she never will. Writing a partial requires different skills from developing a plot, pacing a story and sustaining reader interest through 50 000, 60 000 or 100 000 words.

Even more daunting for the abovementioned writer is the prospect of submitting a manuscript to a publisher. They could reject it. She could fail. Sure, she may not win the competitions she enters but somehow it isn't the same. The judges aren't always professional people and they certainly aren't putting a publisher's money on the line.

This is why winning a competition isn't always an entree to publication. Different skills are required in the writing and different standards are used in assessing the results.

Lack of time—or interest?

Lack of interest can sometimes be disguised as a shortage of time. There's always something more pressing keeping you from writing. Family commitments must come first. Society's needs take precedence. These excuses are so laudable that we may even get brownie points for using them. In fact, if we *don't* use them we may be accused of selfishness and heart-lessness, so they are easy excuses to use.

But have you noticed how you make time for the things you *want* to do? A columnist I know has always wanted to write a novel but never had the time. Yet he bought a huge dog and was able to take it to obedience classes once a week.

This writer publishes in newspapers all over Australia six or seven days a week, so where did the time come from to train the dog? The simple answer is that he *made* time for it because it was something he really wanted to do. Writing a novel was something he thought he *should* do, but he wasn't really committed to it.

Realising this takes a lot of soul-searching and sometimes a heartbreaking amount of self-honesty, but it can save you from a lifetime of misery if you let it.

Not everyone is cut out to be a writer. At school we're taught to string words together with reasonable facility and these days we have computers to handle the drudge work with ease, so writing looks deceptively accessible. It looks like something any idiot ought to be able to do if they tried.

Surprise, surprise, it's not.

Professional writing, no matter what you call it and what markets you aim for, is as demanding and difficult as any other artistic pursuit, be it sculpting, painting, composing music or singing arias. You wouldn't expect to spend your spare weekends dashing off the odd concerto. You wouldn't even try an aria without many years of training and disciplined practice. Writing is no different.

It's OK not *to write*

I suppose I'm saying it's OK *not* to write if you find you don't enjoy it as much as you expected to. It's also fine to write for non-paying markets and small presses or for your own amusement. Painters find it perfectly acceptable to dabble in art and produce unspectacular pictures for their living room walls. Yet for some reason writing isn't considered acceptable unless it's for publication.

There are many kinds of writing you can do which don't impose the demands of writing for publication. You can read your work to small workshop groups. You can enter competitions for the pleasure of competing.

You can self-publish. For many years this was a dirty word, but as publishers become what Morris West calls *agglomerated* and mainly interested in potential blockbuster novels, small presses are making a comeback. Desktop publishing and home photocopiers have put self-publication within the reach and budget of almost anyone. And surprisingly, small-press publication occasionally leads to big-time success.

John Grisham, the best-selling author of *The Firm* and *The Client*, had his first novel, *A Time to Kill*, rejected by 28 publishers. It was finally accepted and 5000 copies were printed. Grisham bought 1000 of them and toured the USA in his van trying to sell them himself.

Today a first edition of that book is worth $4000 and Grisham laughs at the realisation that he carried around in his van about $4 million worth of his books. In contrast to his early struggles, he recently sold the film rights to his latest novel on the strength of two paragraphs of plot outline.

Maybe you'll never emulate John Grisham. Few writers do, even the most successful of them, because there is always an element of luck in stories like his, along with the talent and hard work.

The point is, you don't *have* to emulate Grisham or anyone else. Just decide at the outset that your aim is to enjoy playing with words, putting them together in whatever form takes your fancy, and that you don't care whether they're published or not.

Take the pressure off

Sometimes, taking the pressure off yourself in this way can have unexpected results. Albert Facey's book *A Fortunate Life* was supposedly never meant for publication. It was written to share his experiences with his family, and when they took it to Fremantle Arts Press, they only meant to have some copies printed for the family's use. The rest, as they say, is history.

I can't help wondering if Bert Facey would have felt as comfortable sitting down to chronicle his experiences if he'd thought, 'This had better be good if it's to be a best-seller'. Would he have seen the project through or would he have been too inhibited to go ahead?

Telling other people your writing plans can impose this kind of pressure, but it can be used in different ways. If you seriously want to complete a book and submit it to a publisher, sharing your plans with others can give you the impetus to keep going. When well-meaning friends ask you how the book's going, you will want to have some progress to report. But if you aren't sure this is what you want to do, either keep the news to yourself or state your intentions at the outset: 'I'm trying my hand at writing a book and I won't know till it's done whether I can do it or not.' Then you all know where you stand.

It's only comparatively recently that we've turned the description *amateur* into something resembling a criticism. The word comes from the Latin *amator*, meaning a lover of something, and really describes one who does something for the love of it rather than for payment.

Perhaps we should create a new avocation such as lay-writer to describe one who writes for enjoyment with no more intention of becoming a professional than the model plane builder has of piloting a jumbo jet. Lay-writers would assess themselves by different standards and there would be no 'failure' or 'rejection' to worry about. Imagine someone failing the building of a model plane, or having their efforts rejected!

Fear of failure

This is a larger obstacle to success because it disguises itself in so many ways. The American writer Erica Jong said that for years she never finished a writing project. As long as it remained work in progress it couldn't be rejected.

In our family we tell a story we call The Petrol Man:

> Late one night a motorist ran out of fuel on a lonely road and decided to walk back to a garage he'd passed some time before. As he walked he worried. It was late. The garage owner wouldn't like being woken up. He might become angry and abusive and refuse to help. By the time the motorist reached the garage he was convinced the owner would abuse him. A fight might result. It would be terrible. When the sleepy garage owner opened the door in answer to the knock, before he could say a word the motorist threw the petrol can at him and said, 'You know what you can do with your petrol.'

If we find ourselves responding to imaginary criticisms and problems before they arise, we tell each other to 'stop playing petrol man'.

In writing as in life, most people fear rejection, sometimes going as far as the petrol man and reacting before the world has a chance to assess our work. I was once asked how you know, when you start writing, that you can do it. The answer is that no-one knows for sure. You write to find out *if* you can do it. This means not allowing fear of failure to prevent you from getting started or from finishing the job.

Too often new writers assume that the books they see on the stands came out of the typewriter that way. This couldn't be further from the truth. In *The Writing of One Novel*, Irving Wallace tells of rewriting the ending of *The Prize* three times before it was published. I heard Colleen McCullough tell an audience of writers how her publishers, Harper & Row, asked her to beef up the role of a minor character and change the ending of *The Thorn Birds* before the book was published. Some time ago I was interviewed on the same television show as the playwright Ray Lawler, and he explained that he is *still* revising *Summer of the Seventeenth Doll*—even though it is now regarded as an Australian classic.

It pays to remember that editing is not criticism but an attempt by everyone concerned to produce the best possible work. Even when it involves excising your most cherished words and phrases it must be done. The mistake lies in trying to edit your work before you complete the first draft.

The critic over your shoulder

Writing with an imaginary critic watching over your shoulder is inhibiting but very common. Once you rid yourself of the idea that you must get it right first go, it's easier to focus on the right-brain function of saying what you want to say. You can quiet your critical left brain by assuring it that you will come back and polish the actual words in subsequent drafts, but not right now, thank you.

Len Deighton calls this kind of writing 'a muddled system of trial and error', and it works for him. He says the most difficult lesson to learn is that thousands of words must be discarded. Unfortunately you have to write them before you know which ones they are. I wish I could recall which wit defined a first draft as 'waste paper'. To soften the blow, Deighton says, he keeps his early drafts on a shelf for months before throwing them away. If nothing else, this gives the writer the objectivity which is nearly always lacking when the pages are freshly printed out.

The courage to be wrong

As Alexander Pope said, 'Never be ashamed of being wrong because admitting it is admitting that you are wiser today than yesterday.'

The only way to become wiser today than yesterday is to take a chance and risk making mistakes. Trust yourself to be more creative than you've allowed yourself to be until now, even if you still have doubts. The doubts will probably always be there, but they needn't show in your writing and they should never prevent you from making the attempt.

We've already seen how it's impossible to hold more than one thought in your mind at the same time. It's also impossible to believe two opposing things at once. By changing what you consciously tell yourself about your writing, you can also, in time, change your beliefs.

Beliefs *can* be changed. Many years ago it was considered a 'fact' that peasants couldn't learn to read and write. In the fifteenth century the printing press was invented and this 'fact' was shown for what it was, a myth created by economic circumstances and lack of opportunity. For many years arithmetic was believed to be a magical art understandable only to a few initiates. Samuel Johnson supposedly had a hard time learning this arcane art. One wonders what he would make of the calculators used by practically every western schoolchild today.

It's as if we carry an observer in our heads deciding which bits of reality we'll accept and which we will reject. Reality has very little to do with it, as the above examples illustrate.

Seeing what we want or expect to see extends to many areas of life. Our pupils tend to dilate when we look at something we want to see, and contract when faced with an unwelcome sight. Poor children have been known to perceive coins as larger in size than children who are well off. Decide to go on a diet and immediately you will seem to be surrounded by advertisements for fattening foods. The frequency of the commercials hasn't changed, only your perception of them.

In workshops, I use the following sentence to show how perception can alter what is really there. Quickly count the number of times the letter F appears in this statement:

FEATURE FILMS ARE THE RE-
SULT OF YEARS OF SCIENTI-
FIC STUDY COMBINED WITH
THE EXPERIENCE OF YEARS

Some people count three, others four or five. Very few see the correct number, which is six. The eye tends to skip over the Fs at the beginning of the first and third lines and the ones in the word *of*, which are sounded as Vs.

Once you are able to separate perception from reality you can learn to trust all the levels of your mind to do what you want, just as at night you trust yourself to remember to breathe while you sleep. Most skills are one-tenth mastering the skill and nine-tenths trusting yourself to do it. Very often you don't trust yourself to put the words on paper because you tell yourself it won't work, you'll fail, you'll be ridiculed and so on. In other words, you play petrol man before the first word is even written. Sometimes the petrol man's message is so strong that the words never get written and we live lives of 'quiet desperation', making excuses for not writing but really lacking the courage to take the first steps.

Banish the 'shoulds'

Many of the injunctions which prevent you from getting started come from the area of personality which Transactional Analysis calls *parent*. This is not a real parent but an aggregate of shoulds and oughts accumulated from parents, teachers and other authority figures during our formative years.

The voice of your internal parent is the one telling you you *should* finish what you start, get it right first time, always do your best. Since nearly all writing is rewriting, it's almost impossible to do any of these things at the same time as you create a first draft. The result can be a full-blown case of performance anxiety which prevents you from reaching your writing goals.

The solution is to give yourself permission to write badly. This is not as reckless as it sounds. You won't run amok at the keyboard. You may well have the first fun you've ever had writing. Even at school there was invariably someone leaning over your shoulder correcting your spelling or handwriting. This time you can resolve to banish all those parental figures with their shoulds and oughts, and give yourself permission to write any old how, purely to please yourself.

When students are given this permission in workshops, a strange thing often happens. They begin writing hesitantly, trying not to care how the words come out and to focus only on what they want to say. But out of this exercise comes some of the clearest, cleanest writing they've ever achieved. By deliberately not trying to write *well* and simply writing to communicate, they manage to do both.

One of the least understood aspects of writing seems to me to be the role of the words themselves. I believe they should disappear from the page. The reader should be unaware of their presence and should be caught up in the story being told. The words are the vehicles which carry the reader into the writing. If they draw attention to themselves instead, they aren't doing their job.

Remember, today's disaster is tomorrow's 'so what?'. I have a sign which reads, 'Today is the day you worried about yesterday and all is well.' Many of the things we fear never happen. If and when they do is time enough to deal with them. Playing the petrol man is a complete waste of your precious time. Even if your writing *is* ridiculed or rejected, is it really the end of the world? At least you've had the courage to put your thoughts down on paper and stuck with the task to the end. Half the journalists I know have unfinished novels stuck in their desk drawers. They won't be ridiculed or rejected, but neither will they know the joy of holding a finished book in their hands.

The ice-ball challenge

Years ago I read an article which said that in a few million years the sun will become a nova and the earth, deprived of the sun's warmth, will turn into a ball of ice incapable of supporting life as we know it. Discussing this idea in workshops, I've found there are generally two responses. The pessimists look glum and say, 'What's the use of anything if that's how we're all going to end up?' and the optimists look relieved and say, 'In that case, why worry about the future? We can try anything, take any risk, because in a few million years it won't matter anyway.'

The conclusions are basically the same—nothing we do now will matter in a few million years. But just as you have the option of looking at a glass as half-full or half-empty, you have the choice of seeing the ice-ball theory as an excuse not to try anything, or as a reason why you can dare everything—because ultimately you can't fail.

In a nutshell

1   Nobody ever has all the time, money and ideas they need before they start writing.
2   Create your own deadlines and stick to them. The more time you have for a project, the longer it will take.
3   Recognise that the two main things blocking you are fear of failure and lack of real interest. You don't have to write for publication if it doesn't suit you.
4   Remember the petrol man. Don't let fear of failure deter you from trying to write.
5   Write first, then edit, not both together.
6   Give yourself permission to write badly and concentrate on what you want to say.
7   Use the ice-ball challenge as a reason to dare anything. In a few million years it won't matter anyway, so ultimately you can't fail.

7

The perfectionist trap

Trying to write the perfect book is a sure way to get nothing done. What if it doesn't come out perfect but only so-so? Are you the best judge? At different times two students attended my workshops, each convinced that the only books worth writing were best-sellers. They could see no point in writing 'just another book'.

Unfortunately it is history that makes these judgments, not we writers. The best anyone can hope to do is to analyse a large number of best-selling books and identify common denominators. Using this approach, Hollywood has produced some amazingly expensive flops.

If life is indeed what happens to you while you're making other plans, then a best-seller is what happens to an ordinary manuscript when the author pours heart and soul into it and their passion communicates itself to millions of readers.

If you put off writing because you fear your work won't be good enough, the *only* solution is to plunge in and write those crucial first words. Remember Grenville's Law—it can all be fixed tomorrow. Abandon the idea that what you write must be perfect on the first or even the 51st attempt. Concentrate on what you want to say or the story you want to tell. Let your passion and commitment carry you away and there's a good chance they will have the same effect on your readers.

Five steps you can take

Here are five steps you can take to overcome the trap of perfectionism:

1   *Write it anyway*
    Put a sign above your desk which says IT'S OK TO BE WRONG. Avoid apologising in advance when showing your work to others or in query letters to publishers. Don't say it's *only* a first draft or *only* anything. Let the work stand on its own merits. Most importantly, don't preface the work with 'You may not like this but . . .'.

2   *Let other people write things their way*
    One of the toughest editing skills to master is the ability to leave someone else's writing alone. Teach yourself to recognise the distinction between writing something

better and writing it differently. If your version is merely different but not necessarily better, have the courage to hand the work back untouched. In business there's a tendency to make changes simply to show you're doing your job. Try putting a positive comment on the work and initial it. Encourage others to do the same. Avoid change for change's sake.

3   *Stop asking for advice*

More writing is robbed of what Ernest Hemingway called its 'juice' by well-meaning advice than by most other influences combined. If you're a beginner, by all means take classes and attend workshops and critique sessions until you master the basic techniques of writing. These are learnable skills which you need to know just as a carpenter must learn to mitre a corner or chamfer a board. But sooner or later you have to write your stories your way.

If you do seek advice, ask for specific help. Instead of asking what someone thinks of your work, ask them where they thought it was slow or unclear. Ask them how they reacted to the main character, when they suspected who the murderer was, and so on. This relieves them of the burden of deciding your story's fate and shows them how they can be of help.

The same applies to critique groups and can save a lot of time arguing over what are basically differences of opinion. Some writers make up their own 'critique sheets' to accompany their work. The editor or critique group is invited to tick boxes indicating such things as 'pacing OK/too slow/too fast', 'conflict clear/not clear' and so on.

4   *Live in the present, not the past*

Like the writers I know who carry around one polished project for the rest of their careers, it's tempting to live on past glories but it's more productive if you look to your next piece of work as your most important.

5   *Write your work your way*

Just because a close friend writes murder mysteries, don't feel you must do the same. Your forte may be historical romance or science fiction. This also applies to writing for money. If you are a poet at heart you may have to resign yourself to making very little money but satisfying your own creative needs. Writing for money seldom works and almost every publisher will tell you that financial rewards usually only arrive after several years of hard work and consistent output. By trusting yourself to do your own work in your own way, you open yourself to more original ideas because you're not constantly at odds with your inner needs.

Following these steps may seem scary at first, a bit like walking a tightrope without a safety net underneath, but the more you apply the steps the stronger will become your faith in yourself and your ability to have and develop good ideas.

A psychologist friend of mine suggests using your fears as a springboard to greater understanding of yourself. If you find you're uncomfortable sending off a story to a magazine without first showing it to several friends for comment, ask yourself what it is that you're really afraid of.

Usually it will be one or more of these three:

- being wrong
- ridicule
- actual loss

The second fear is often seen as a consequence of the first: if you write something stupid (fear of failure), it will be read by everyone in the world and they will laugh at you (fear of ridicule). For a start, even in these days of the global village there is no medium so far-reaching that *everyone* you know will read it. Even after publishing over 50 books with sales of more than 15 million copies around the world, the first question I'm asked at parties is generally 'What name do you write under?' Translation—if you're so great, why haven't I heard of you?

What you're really concerned about is that your close family and friends will read your work and judge you harshly. Practically every writer suffers pangs of anxiety when they first realise that their mother might be reading their work. This is because we have internalised the 'parent' mentioned previously, that combination of shoulds and oughts which we carry around in our heads. It can be daunting enough to prevent you from writing altogether if you let it.

One way to overcome these fears is to behave as you would if your real parent criticised some aspect of your adult life. Would you thank them for the input and do your own thing anyway? Most grown-ups do. Applying this approach to your written work may help. If the authority figures in your life were particularly harsh and critical it may be a tough step to take, but it's worth making the effort.

Trying something new will nearly always leave you open to fear of failure, and such fear is far from unfounded. You *could* fail. The work *may* be rejected by an editor or publisher. But mainly this 'petrol man' attitude comes from your own self-doubts. For example, if you are uncertain of your own intelligence you may fear that others will find you stupid. Acknowledging the fear and going ahead anyway is often the only solution. Writing blocks may be a defence against the pain of criticism and failure, and for a time they work, but if you let them get the better of you you'll eventually have to deal with an even greater pain, that of your own unfulfilled creativity.

If it helps, remember that you are not your work, nor will you be judged on any one piece of writing. Even the most successful writers produce a real dud now and then, either because their judgment is off or because they are in love with a particular idea and don't much care whether others appreciate it or not. These unappreciated ideas are often the ones later described as 'sleepers', which become best-sellers when reading tastes eventually catch up.

Fear of actual loss may be easier to deal with because it is a concrete worry and can be dealt with in a concrete manner. Start by asking yourself, 'What's the worst that can happen?'

You can fail. In this case you can resolve to be like Thomas Edison, who tried nearly 2000 versions of his filament light bulb before he perfected it. When he was asked how he regarded so many failures, he said he now knew 2000 things which didn't work. He chose to see each failure as a step closer to his goal.

You can choose to see each rejection slip from an editor or publisher as proof that you are actively pursuing your writing ambitions. Take particular note of any slips that carry specific editorial comments. They are proof that you are making progress.

It is not well known, but when romance publishers Harlequin Mills & Boon send out rejection letters, the longer the letter, the closer the writer has come to acceptance. This may seem contradictory. Doesn't a long letter of criticism mean there are more things wrong with the work? Yes, but it also means the editor was sufficiently interested in this writer to spend valuable time making constructive comments. It's intended as encouragement because the editor knows that a determined writer will be like Thomas Edison, using the comments as stepping-stones to eventual acceptance.

You can also ask yourself what's the worst actual loss you can sustain. Luckily for writers, the investment is mainly one of time rather than money. You can't open a business without investing a great deal in leases, fitments, documentation and stock. But a writer can set up shop with a keyboard, some paper and a spare corner of a room. You can even 'moonlight' while gaining income from your regular job. One wag suggested using the spare time at work to write on the grounds that he was making his employer a patron of the arts. I'm not sure how many employers would agree, but it does show how easily a writer can get started.

Naturally you'll need money for stationery and postage, but the amounts are modest and most hobbies would involve some cash outlay.

When to give up your day job

More challenging is the decision to become a full-time writer. This decision usually looms when you are selling enough work to provide a spare-time income which is not yet enough to live on, but which could be if you were able to write full-time.

One solution is to reverse your present situation. Take a part-time job and write full-time. Many writers are surprised to find that their output, far from increasing with the extra time, either decreases under the pressure of *having* to write, or stays about the same as when they were writing part-time.

This happened to me when I made the transition from freelance journalist to romance writer. Part-time, I produced three novels a year. Full-time, my output wasn't much greater, for two reasons: I was more conscious of the need for quality writing, as my living depended on it; and I had exhausted my store of available ideas in the previous three years of working part-time. The slow-down would have occurred anyway, but I was more conscious of it because my expectations of myself had increased with the switch to full-time novel writing.

There are ways you can prepare yourself and lessen the fear of actual loss. Decide a year in advance that you are going to take a certain amount of time to try to write full-time, and save as hard as you can against that time. Decide how long you can afford to live on your savings and set that period aside as writing time, less a couple of months for job-hunting in case it's needed.

If you're lucky enough to have some weeks or months of leave accrued, you could use this time to test yourself as a full-time writer. Give yourself a brief vacation period, then settle down to write as if it were your living. Keep the same hours and routine as you would if the rent depended on it. Often as little as a month of this will tell you whether the writing life is for you.

At the same time, re-read the section on lack of interest and establish whether writing is something you want and need to do or something you think sounds good to talk about at parties. If it's the latter, simply stop dreaming about being a full-time writer and berating yourself for not producing more. As you'll discover if you give it a month's trial, writing isn't a substitute for an easy life, or a kind of respectable retirement. It's mostly sheer hard slog, with occasional bright moments of feverish inspiration and flattering invitations to appear on TV talk shows.

There are two more hazards you should be aware of, no matter what kind of writing you want to do. They are:

- saturation
- the sequence trap

Saturation

Just as it's true that we know more than we know we know, the reverse can also be true—we know less than we think.

If your partner disappeared today, would you be able to tell the police what they were wearing when last you saw them? If a friend who normally wears a moustache were to shave it off, how long would it take you to notice?

Here's a quick test of your observation skills. If you normally wear a watch, put your watch hand out of sight right now without glancing at it. Now draw a rough sketch of your watch face. This isn't a test of artistic skill but of observation. Are the numbers on your watch generated electronically or printed on? Does it have Roman or ordinary numerals? A second hand or not? What brand markings are on it and where are they located on the dial? What colour is your watch face?

If you don't wear a watch, before you start to feel smug, try doing the same exercise with the numbers on a telephone dial. How are they set out? Where is the zero located? Now compare the reality with your sketch. How well did you do?

Don't be surprised if you found this exercise a challenge. Practically everybody does, including me, even after having set it as a workshop exercise on dozens of occasions.

This is saturation in action. We look at so many things but we don't always see them accurately, yet this is a quality

Draw your watch

a writer must cultivate in order to transpose the real world onto the printed page.

Overcome the saturation trap

The best way to do this is to train yourself to look at life through a writer's eyes. Teach yourself to see and hear what's around you much more accurately.

Eavesdropping is a splendid way to hone your dialogue-writing skills. People from different backgrounds and occupations speak differently. If you've ever bought a house you'll recognise that 'handyman's dream' means one thing to a real estate agent and quite another to a potential purchaser.

Keeping a diary or notebook will also enable you to record your impressions accurately. You can use it to keep track of ideas, snatches of overheard conversation, and descriptive passages. My friend the late Mary Drake, author of 300 stories, kept diaries without missing a day for 60 years. Material from them formed the basis of her autobiography *The Trees Were Green*.

Seeing life through a writer's eyes can have its drawbacks. Many writers report the sensation of living life on two levels, as observer and participant. I have caught myself, in the midst of grief, noting my own reactions, and wondered if this made me insincere. Now I know it makes me a writer. Once I was hypnotised and told under hypnosis that I wouldn't recall the session but would awaken feeling refreshed and energised. I went home and wrote a detailed account of the whole experience in case it should come in handy.

Hemingway urged writers to train themselves by minutely observing everyday occurrences such as a fish jumping on the end of a line:

> Remember what the action was that gave you the
> excitement. Then write it down, making it clear so the
> reader will see it too and have the same feeling you had.

The sequence trap

In life things tend to happen in orderly, predictable ways. The order in which things happen changes them. If you are poor and become rich you will behave differently from someone who is rich and loses all their money. If you marry more than once your attitudes and behaviour towards your second partner will be coloured by your experiences with your first partner.

All human experience tends to be sequential, but this doesn't mean you have to be locked in by the original information if new information comes to hand which changes what you 'knew' before. This is what Edward de Bono calls 'the sequence trap' and it is a powerful obstacle to creative thinking because it tends to limit what we permit ourselves to see.

Comedians recognise this and use it to surprise us with the punchlines of jokes like this one: The last bald eagle went in search of a mate and took another bird back to his nest. The other bird kept the eagle awake all night calling, 'I'm a loon and I love to spoon. I'm a loon and I love to spoon.' Driven crazy, the eagle sent the loon away and brought another bird back to the nest. This bird spent all night cooing, 'I'm a dove and I like to make love. I'm a dove and I like to make love.' Infuriated, the eagle threw the dove out and brought another prospective mate back to the nest. This time it was a duck and it said, 'I'm a drake, you made a mistake.'

The joke sets up the expectation that the next bird will also rhyme its statement, this time with 'duck'; the laugh comes from the surprise we get when the sequence is broken.

The old adage 'If it ain't broke, don't fix it' could be applied to the way we regard the sequence trap. If a decision or a step already made is working, why would we want to re-evaluate it? But progress isn't always a matter of changing things that are wrong. Sometimes it means replacing things that have become obsolete even though they were right for their time.

There's no such thing as absolute rightness. Any idea, no matter how right, may need another look in time. To avoid the sequence trap you need to get into the habit of surveying the steps you've taken and the decisions you've made to see if they're still the right ones, given your current knowledge and experience.

Change without tears

If you have set your sights on writing film scripts but find your talents are better suited to writing children's books, you should be able to make the change without undue distress. Some people are too afraid of what others might think. Yet a change of career can be the best thing to happen to you, as was the case with Colonel Harland Sanders, who discovered his knack for frying chicken in retirement.

Building on what's gone before—sequentially—may not always be the best way to go. Writers often think in terms of 'starting small' by writing short stories or children's books before tackling adult fiction. One has only to attempt the shorter media to realise that they are not the 'shallow end' of the writing pool but separate pools entirely, with their own shoals and hidden obstacles.

At the same time, if you try one of these fields and discover you have a talent for it, there is nothing wrong with staying in that field and developing to the best of your ability. Don't feel you are betraying some imaginary ideal by not 'moving on' to a novel if short stories prove to be your forte.

This doesn't mean you can't experiment with other fields of writing. By all means try your hand at as many as interest you until you discover where your talents lie. But don't let the sequence trap distract you from what gives you and your readers fulfilment and pleasure.

The research trap

A variation on the sequence trap is the research trap, which so immobilises many writers that they are unable to escape it and actually write anything.

Information usually comes to us a bit at a time. We can't wait until we have all the information we need before deciding what to do next. For example, when making a career choice, it isn't possible to know the whole future of a given industry. In writing, it's still perfectly possible to invest time developing a book for a particular publisher's line only to find that by the time your manuscript is ready, the line has been discontinued. This is one reason why I encourage writers to market their work in partial form as soon as they feel confident they can complete the project. Writing several sample chapters, a synopsis and a query letter will take far less time than finishing a manuscript. It also reduces the chance that major changes will take place at your chosen publishers before you've shown them your book.

One of the most difficult areas to know when enough is enough is in historical research. Researching an entire era can seem overwhelming at first. The solution is not to try. Read enough about your chosen period that you feel comfortable about it and no more. This may take half a dozen books or more. The same applies when you're researching a non-fiction subject. The first book you read will be all new to you. You'll probably tell yourself you'll never know enough about the subject to write about it convincingly. Persevere. By the second, third and fourth books you'll begin to notice overlapping themes and subject matter. You'll begin to feel a slight familiarity with the overall thrust of the subject or historical period.

That's where you stop for now. It doesn't mean you won't be doing any more research, but it's enough for the moment.

Your next step is to develop the project in very rough overview form based on your newly acquired feel for the subject matter. This will have a curious effect. It will nearly always show you exactly where you need to do further research so you can narrow your study to these areas rather than try to wade through everything ever written on a given topic.

Even then it will be necessary to start writing before your research is complete. But recognise that over-researching can be a form of procrastination, of appearing to work on a project rather than taking the scary step of starting the actual writing.

The solution is to start writing the first draft, making it as rough as you please. Whenever you come across something you need to research further, put an asterisk or star at that point, or the printer's mark t/c, meaning 'to come'. This saves you having to switch out of the creative right brain into the research-oriented left brain every time you become aware of a missing piece of information.

It may help if you bear in mind that no-one ever has all the information they need before starting a writing project. There's always another book you could read, another telephone call you could make or interview you could conduct, but recognise these as traps. If you still find it impossible to start writing, ask yourself whether the idea is as fully developed as it ought to be. In other words, is it ready to be written? This is a different problem from the sequence trap described above. The answer will probably only become apparent after you've tried all the sequence-breaking steps described. If you're still blocked, it may be what Marshall Cook called in *Writer's Digest* 'a message from your muse telling you an idea isn't quite ready yet'.

Everyone's a critic

Another common block to creative thinking is *prejudging*. Judging everything, including ideas, is a habit. The world is full of 'no' people who are ready to tell you why your idea won't work. In an insurance company I saw a poster which said 'There are no yes-men in this company. We say no when the boss does.'

As an experiment, try this test on some friends. Announce, for example, you're thinking of leaving the city and moving to the country. Then sit back. What sort of comments are you likely to receive? Generally most would be well-meaning but negative, pointing out all the potential pitfalls of such a move. Some of the problems pointed out might include the isolation, the expense of relocation, the difficulty of obtaining employment, the loss of friends and social life and so on.

If the idea is a serious one and you want input, you can try the same process on your own, writing down all the reasons why your plan won't work. Put these on one side of a sheet of paper.

Now ask the same group of friends to give you some reasons why your idea might be a *good* one. Ask them to pretend for a moment that your plan is worth considering, even if they don't fully believe it yet. You're thinking of relocating to the country. What might be some of the positive aspects? If you're working alone, write your answers on the other side of your sheet of paper.

Some of the advantages might include peace and quiet, lower cost of living, the ability to purchase a better house for the same investment, fewer distractions and so on. Notice how some of the positive reasons for the move are exactly the same as the negative ones but seen from a different perspective?

Forcing yourself and others to consider both sides of an argument enables you to gain a more balanced view. If you're in business and surrounded by 'no' people you can do the same exercise. After they've exhausted all the reasons why a proposal won't work, ask them to look at some of the reasons why it might be worthwhile. It's a challenge few people can resist. Nobody wants to sit in a meeting like a dummy, so they will generally put the same energy into the yes case as into the no case.

If you've ever participated in a formal debate you'll recognise the similarities. In a debate you aren't always given the choice of which side you'll support. Forcing yourself to look at both sides of an argument can have unexpected benefits. It can temper the enthusiasm we all have for our own ideas, which can prevent us from seeing possible pitfalls. And it can be a great aid to decision-making.

Tomorrowitis

Another common block which prevents more books from being written than all the others combined is *tomorrowitis*. Everyone suffers from it at some time, but whether it's a passing virus or a terminal illness is up to you. Remember Henry Ford's maxim: you can't build a reputation on what you're *going* to do.

In Eugene O'Neill's play *The Iceman Cometh*, the character Harry Hope always intends to take a walk around the block. He has every intention of going out. But he's too busy, the weather is bad, his rheumatism is bothering him. Harry comes up with dozens of reasons to postpone his walk until tomorrow and, of course, tomorrow never comes. As the play progresses we realise that Harry has been postponing his walk for 20 years. Are there things in your life you've been postponing like Harry's walk? What about the life story only you can write; the sales manual which capitalises on your years of experience in selling; the play; the poem; the children's story?

The trouble with tomorrow is that it never comes. But tomorrowitis is like many of the other blocks, a habit which can be broken. The more you put things off, the harder they become to do.

The symptoms are easily recognised.

I've been too busy.
I haven't had a chance.
I'll do it when I get time.
I have more pressing commitments.
They need this done first.
I'll relax first, then start.

Do you find yourself using expressions like these? If they're a normal part of your vocabulary they could be the biggest block to your creativity.

Drilling in the permafrost

You've probably heard the expression 'If you want something done, ask a busy person.' Why is that? The people who drill for oil way up north in the permafrost know that if they let the drill stop for more than a few minutes at a time it will ice up and be impossible to start again. It will become rigid and snap when they try to reuse it.

What does a busy person have in common with drilling in the permafrost? It's a thing called *momentum*, the forward thrust which keeps you warmed up and ticking over, ready to start the next project almost before you've cleared your desk from the last one. If you're to develop this momentum, you must get into the habit of doing what you say you will when you say it. The truth is, people who are successful don't write because they are inspired—they become inspired because they're writing.

I call this *push starting*. As with a car, once you develop momentum it's easier to keep going. The hard part is getting started.

A small way to practise developing momentum costs practically nothing except time and effort. Make an agreement with yourself that you will always deliver on your promises, no matter what.

If you casually promise to send a friend a newspaper cutting, write a note to yourself the moment you make the promise. Keep your note in your wallet or purse or anywhere you'll come across it when you get home. Then as soon as you come across the note, *act on it*. If you make small promises to friends but rarely deliver, this is one habit you can change and it will help you to develop momentum in your working life.

Like continuous drilling in the permafrost, it will keep you warmed up and ticking over, changing your view of yourself from someone who's going to do things, to someone who does them. At the very least it will make you think twice before making idle promises.

What does this have to do with your creativity? It frees your mind to do what's important instead of letting it get bogged down in life's busywork.

The fear factor

Sometimes, without realising it, we make a choice to get bogged down in life's details because it's easier than facing the task we're dodging. The book isn't getting written not because I might fail, but because I have all these family commitments to honour. Like the busy writer who found time to take his dog to obedience classes, you need to carefully and honestly examine your situation. Is lack of time really the problem? What else is going on here?

We've already looked at fear of failure and lack of real interest. If neither of those is the problem, what else might be holding you back? Are you qualified for what you want to write? Do you need more information? Is there a course you can take, a book you could buy and read, or someone you could talk with to fill in the gaps?

Break down your project into bite-sized pieces. Every book is written one word at a time. Choose some small step you can do right away. Maybe you can think of a title for your book. How about a stunning opening sentence? Once you begin, you will develop the momentum that keeps you going. Then you'll be drilling in the permafrost of your writing life—and who knows, you may even strike oil.

In a nutshell

1 'Write it anyway.' There's no such thing as a perfect book or the perfect moment to write.
2 Stop seeking advice. Write your work your way.
3 Train yourself to really see what's around you and avoid the saturation trap.
4 Try different kinds of writing to see what suits you. No

one kind of writing is inherently better than another, despite the sequence trap.

5   Research just enough to feel comfortable, then start writing and fill in the gaps later.

6   Explore both sides of every question to avoid the habit of *pre-judging*.

7   Drill in the permafrost of your ideas and keep going until you build up momentum.

8   Recognise tomorrowitis as fear of failure in disguise.

8

What's your problem?

A boastful individual announced to a friend that he was giving up half of his sex life. Which half, asked the friend—talking about it or thinking about it?

Theory is all very well, but it's like this person's sex life, no good unless it is put into practice. In this section we're going to examine how to use creative methods to solve problems so you can be sure of having more ideas than you can ever use. We'll also touch on four tools you can use to develop those ideas, and how you can generate more of those Eureka moments when the answer you seek comes to you seemingly 'out of the blue'.

Solving problems creatively can take many forms. You can try the approach used by the two mountaineers. One of them fell and broke both his arms and legs. His companion wanted to pull him back up the mountain. Thinking creatively, he suggested the injured climber hold the rope between his teeth. This worked well and the companion was able to haul his friend slowly up to safety. 50 metres, 40 metres, 30, 20, 10 . . . until the friend was in sight. The climber at the top called down, 'Are you OK?' The injured climber called back, 'Ye-e-e-e-e-s.' Which means that either your mother was right and you shouldn't talk with your mouth full, or you need to take many factors into account when solving problems creatively.

In workshops I've evolved a formula which helps to ensure that these factors are taken into account. It's called ISISI—pronounced I-see-I-see.

The steps are:

Identify
Survey
Ideation
Selection
Implementation

Identify the problem

This is possibly the most important step to take, although it isn't always as obvious as it seems. There's a real temptation to skip this stage, and the next one, and go straight to the ideation stage, the part with all the *sanuk*. But first you need to be sure that the problem you're solving is the right one.

In the United States, engineers were faced with the problem of how to create a mechanical tomato picker. Nothing they tried worked, until it was realised that the problem lay not with the picker but with the tomato. By breeding a tougher-skinned tomato which grew lower on the bush, they were able to pick it more efficiently using available methods.

Sandbags have been used for a long time to hold back floodwater but they can cause problems with filling, handling and storage, especially during dry periods. Then when it floods it's difficult to locate large supplies of sand, people to fill the bags and heavy labour to manhandle them into place. Again, the problem is not managing the sandbags, it's how to hold back floodwater effectively. The Japanese solved the problem with characteristic efficiency by developing bags which could be filled with water—of which there is an abundance during flooding—thus using the water against itself.

Space problems

If your present house is overcrowded, you could decide to buy a bigger house. Again, identifying the problem can multiply your options. Is the problem the house itself or lack of space for specific activities? Once you decide on the answer—say you need some space in which to write—you can then look at ways to solve that specific problem.

You might look at creating an attic in roof space which is presently wasted. Or renting a caravan to park in your driveway. One writer solved the problem by placing a board across her laundry tub to provide a desk which she reached using a bar stool as a chair. Renting an office elsewhere may

Freeing up space to write.

also free up space at home which you presently use for writing. It may also boost your productivity, as I found when I rented an office away from my home, which was then a small terrace house. Knowing you have to meet the rent on an office every month has an amazing effect on output. You produce because you have to.

What other alternatives might solve a space problem?

Editing problems

Concentrating on the work the writing has to do is a way of identifying the problem. When asked to change a piece of writing, very often a new writer will simply rewrite the same piece in different words, then wonder why it doesn't work. First you have to decide what work the writing is doing, then find a different and hopefully better way of achieving it.

In the section on seeing UFOS, we looked at the importance to the editing process of identifying what work the writing is doing in the manuscript. Once you know what result you want to achieve, you can follow the rest of the steps in this chapter to find new and more original ways of achieving it.

Personal problems

The ISISI process can also be used to solve personal problems. Again, you start by identifying the problem. If a partner complains that you're spending too much time writing, is this really the problem you're being asked to address? Or is the other person actually saying they feel neglected and left out of this aspect of your life? Behind almost every accusation which begins 'you always' or 'you never' are what might be called 'me statements'. If such complaints are properly defined,

119

they almost always start with 'I feel', as in 'I feel I don't count with you because of the time you spend on your writing.'

Whatever the problem, it helps to probe deeper and try to identify *specifically* what it is about the writing—or whatever—that's causing the difficulty.

Survey the problem's world

The more background you have on the subject, the more options you will have for solving it. At this stage you're mainly seeking information, so it's important to approach this step with an open mind. Don't exclude or judge any information until you've surveyed the whole field of the problem.

For example, if the problem is lack of a writing place at home, you would need to investigate all the options—including building possibilities, council regulations, costs of different alternatives compared with moving costs, the price of more spacious accommodation, rental charges for caravans, and any other factors that might enter into the decision.

You might also want to investigate office rents and availability in your area. Find out everything you can about the problem. Talk to people who've had the same problem and find out how they solved it. Read some building or decorating magazines, talk to local building advisory centres, go to trade shows and seminars. Fact-finding will help you to become objective about the problem and see beyond your emotional involvement with it.

Part of surveying the problem's world is a process called *incubation*. We'll go into this process more fully in a later chapter, but for now it means simply letting the information you've gathered sit for a while. This gives your right brain time to digest everything you've learned, play with it and experiment with new combinations and ways of dealing with the new knowledge. This is like the 'machine busy' signal you get from a computer. It's time to step back and trust your mind to work on the permutations of the problem while you do something else such as mowing the lawn or catching up on some filing.

Ideation

This is the step most people associate with creativity. It is usually pictured as a light bulb going on over the head or a flash of lightning. While these are useful visual metaphors, they tend to suggest that ideas come from somewhere outside you. In my experience, ideation is an active process during which your brain generates ideas based on the input provided by your survey sessions. In the next chapters, we'll look at the four main ways to generate ideas—tools of the idea trade, if you will. They are brainstorming, clustering, journal keeping and visualisation.

At this stage you want as many ideas as you can get, applying no selectivity at all until the next stage. During the ideation stage, whichever method you use—clustering, brainstorming or whatever—you should use the UFOS technique to make the ideas unlimited, flexible, original . . . and only lastly, specific.

Selection

The next stage in the ISISI process is selection, sorting the ideas you've generated during ideation into some sort of coherent form. This is a left-brain function, which is why it is separated from the right-brain ideation process itself.

How you sort your ideas is up to you. You might number them from 1 to 10 with 1 the most workable and 10 the least practicable. Or you might number them in the order in which you would like to try them out. Another method is the one used by Benjamin Franklin: making a list of the advantages and disadvantages of each idea. He recommended drawing a line down the centre of a sheet of paper and putting the pros on one side and the cons on the other. Sometimes merely seeing which list is the longer is enough to suggest which is the best approach.

Implementation

The final step in the ISISI process is the one frequently overlooked, whether by individuals or committees. Who is going to bell the cat? This comes from Aesop's fable about a committee of mice which got together and decided it would be a good idea to put a bell on the local cat to warn them of its approach. Everyone agreed it was an excellent idea until one lone mouse stood up and asked, 'But who is going to bell the cat?'

It's all very well to have a good idea, but you must have a plan of action to implement it. It's no use dreaming about writing a blockbuster novel or even having a great idea for a plot, unless you have a plan for completing the work. The idea of writing maybe 500 pages is intimidating. But if you write two pages a day, you can finish the project in less than a year. Most writers can manage to produce two pages a day.

If the thought of committing a year to a project concerns you, you might remember the 50-year-old man who told his doctor that he dreamed of studying law. The problem was, he was already 50 and it would take him ten years of part-time study to earn a law degree, by which time he would be 60, and 'too old' to practise law. The doctor asked the man how old he would be then if he didn't study.

Once you reach the implementation stage, resolve not to be like Harry Hope and fulfil your dream 'someday'. Start now. Take some forward step, however small, to establish that all-important momentum to keep yourself energised as you work towards your goal. It's trite but true that the journey of a thousand miles begins with a single step. And as with drilling in the permafrost, the more steps you take the easier it becomes to keep going.

Avoid hardening of the categories

These days there is a tendency to accept solutions based on reason, logic and hard data. Yet many scientists admit that they first reached their conclusions through emotions and 'gut feelings', then worked out the science to back up their feelings.

You can't be original if you suffer from hardening of the categories. We've already seen how the sequence trap works to limit creative thinking and idea generation. Hardening of the categories is its first cousin, the kind of thinking which says all conclusions must be data based. It also says we've always done things this way and can't conceive of a new approach.

Sitting in a friend's kitchen while she cooked a roast one Sunday, I was surprised to see her carefully amputate the shank end of the leg of lamb before putting the dish into the oven. Thinking she knew something I didn't, I asked her why she did it. She explained that her mother and grandmother had always done the same. She didn't know why. But her curiosity was aroused and she asked her mother about it. It turned out that her grandmother had once owned a very small oven. It would only accommodate a leg of lamb if the shank was cut off.

Buttons on the cuffs of men's suits are another example of hardened categories. They were provided in the days before handkerchiefs as a deterrent to using the cuff instead. Yet the buttons are retained long after their usefulness is over.

Similar hardened thinking restricted the development of the first turning indicators on cars. Horse and buggy drivers used to hold out their whips to indicate the direction in which they intended to turn so the first cars had flip-out turning indicators which mimicked the buggy drivers' gestures. It took a leap beyond this categorical thinking to conceive of a blinking light to indicate a driver's intentions.

How else might drivers indicate to others that they intend to turn? Thinking outside the categories might suggest solutions such as panels on the side of the car which glow in the direction of the intended turn. Why not put lights on the *road* which blink on when a car's wheels first cross them? Can you think of other non-hardened alternatives?

Traps such as hardening of the categories can block your attempts to solve problems creatively by putting obstacles in your way which aren't really obstacles at all. A good example is the famous Nine Dots test. The dots are to be joined together using only four straight lines and without lifting your pencil from the paper.

The solution is to extend your four lines well beyond the imaginary square created by the dots. Nowhere in the 'rules' does it say you can't do this, yet surprisingly few people think of going outside the boundary suggested by the dots.

An interior decorator friend of mind solved a very common design problem by thinking beyond the categories. He was faced with a tiny back room which normally would provide space for no more than a single bed and a wardrobe. Using a clever arrangement of built-in furniture he provided facilities for storage, dressing, ironing, guest sleeping quarters and study, all within the same limited space.

His category-breaking solution was similar to the solution of the Nine Dots puzzle—he used the airspace as well as the floor space. Building upwards, he put a guest bed across the top of a wardrobe, accessible by a ladder. Another wardrobe was built across the room, creating a walk-in arrangement to

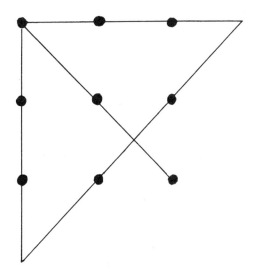

make best use of the floor space, while the study centre fitted under the other furniture.

A combination of hardening of the categories and the sequence trap can be seen in this simple workshop exercise. Participants are asked to list the mistakes in this sentence:

THERE IS THREE ERRERS IN THIS SENTENCE.

Most people quickly spot the spelling mistake and the use of the singular verb 'is' instead of 'are'. But very few manage to see past the message in the sentence to question that there are three errors to be found. In fact, the third error is the presumption itself. If you spotted the third error in the statement itself, congratulations on thinking well outside the boundaries of the exercise.

Again, one way to avoid hardening of the categories when faced with any kind of problem is to focus on the result you need to obtain—or the work the writing has to do. This leads you past the presumptions and assumptions which block creative thinking. Remember my speaker shelves? As soon as I focused on the result needed, which was 'holding up speakers', I was able to consider a whole new range of possibilities.

When it comes to writing, the same rule applies. A friend of mine was plotting a historical novel and needed to have several events, including the Black Death, happen fairly close together. Unfortunately the historical events actually happened some decades apart. He couldn't figure out how to get all three elements he needed into the same time period and still be historically accurate.

He solved the problem by focusing on the result he needed. What work was the Black Death doing in his novel? If it was a way to kill off most members of a character's family, leaving that character alone in the world, there were probably several other historically correct events which would do the same work. He could also use a localised power struggle between opposing parties, a politically motivated raid on the fictional family's home, or any number of alternatives. It then became a case of choosing the most interesting event.

For a writer it's tempting to settle on the first viable solution that comes to mind—hardening of the categories at work. Forcing yourself to push beyond your own mental boundaries—the 'Nine Dots' of everyday thinking—allows you to be far more original. It also pinpoints which scenes are unproductive or 'padding'. These are invariably the passages which an editor will identify as 'slow'. Based on the above method, you should be able to identify the work every word has to do. If not, that passage can safely be edited out.

Questions you can ask to identify these passages include:

- Does this reveal new aspects of character?
- Does it carry the story forward?
- Does it provide or increase conflict?
- Does it add pace, tension or excitement?
- Does it provide new information?

Every scene or passage should do one or more of these things if it is to pull its weight in the manuscript. If the piece *does* do some of this work and needs to be rewritten, going back to basics will show you other ways to rewrite the passage so it still does the same job.

When searching for alternatives, aim to come up with a specific number of choices—say 20—and don't stop until your list is filled. As with any form of idea generation, the first thoughts on your list will be the safe, predictable ones. The next few will be a little more original and interesting and the last few, when you're really working to come up with something, will be the specks of gold in your idea pan.

Next we'll look at some ways to generate those specks of gold.

In a nutshell

1   Use the ISISI (I-see-I-see) formula to solve problems creatively:
    Identify—what is the *real* problem here?
    Survey—learn about the problem's background.
    Ideation—generate as many solutions as you can using the methods in the next chapter.
    Selection—sort ideas into workable form.
    Implementation—create and implement a plan of action to achieve your goals.
2   Recognise how 'hardening of the categories' can block creative thinking.
3   Look past what *is* to see what *might be*—learn to focus on the work you want each piece of writing to do.

9

Tools of the idea trade

When a writer is asked 'Where do you get your ideas?' the real question being asked is '*How* do you get your ideas?' In other words, how does a writer produce something from nothing, a story or a novel seemingly out of thin air? The enquirer often adds, 'I could never do that. I'm not creative like you.'

The same person will then tell you how they adapted a recipe for their family's enjoyment, improvised a costume for a school play out of a pair of curtains, or budgeted for a holiday out of the housekeeping money, without realising that all these activities use the 'creative muscle' which I believe we all possess to a greater or lesser degree.

Like all muscles, this one can be strengthened with exercise and regular use. One reason why writers may be able to conjure up ideas more readily is that they exercise their creative muscle frequently. As someone once said, your mental capacity is no more a given than the size of your biceps. Both can be enlarged and strengthened with the right exercises.

This has been proven in experiments where teachers are told that their students are brighter than average when in truth the children are of normal ability. Treating them as if they were highly intelligent by giving them extra challenges and attention tends to make the belief self-fulfilling.

A creativity work-out

Believing that practice and exercise can make you more creative is the first step. Then you have to put the exercises into practice on a regular basis. Just as an occasional round of the gym won't do more than give you sore muscles, reading these suggestions may arouse your interest but won't do much more. You must get into the habit of stretching your mental muscles at every opportunity.

Even the most mundane decision-making can be used to give your creativity muscle a work-out. Instead of serving the same foods day after day, try out some new recipes. Rearrange your furniture. Try a new filing system. All of the tools in this chapter have one thing in common—they challenge you to seek out and embrace novelty and change. They are like mind steroids which will boost your creativity muscle. As the Roman emperor and sage Marcus Aurelius said, 'The blazing fire makes flames and brightness of everything thrown into it.' Aim to provide your mental furnace with many types of fuel to generate the 'flames and brightness' of original ideas.

The actor Leonard Nimoy believes there is a danger in waiting for opportunity to knock:

> Taken literally this might mean that all one needs to do is sit and listen for the sound of knuckles on wood. My feeling is quite the contrary, and always has been. I believe that it's through the individual's commitment to various ideas and projects that one discovers surprising opportunities. I don't believe there is such a thing as 'a waste of time' involved when a person is pursuing an idea, a project, a hobby, a social cause or whatever motivates him.

He cites an instance where working for a political cause led him to a marvellous acting opportunity. A decision to go to

Spain to take a minor acting role led him to work with Sam Wannamaker which in turn led to a discussion about the Old Globe Theatre and eventually to an enriching production of *The Man in the Glass Booth* which turned out to be a triumph for Nimoy.

Screenwriter William Goldman says he consciously notes details which may come in handy for his future writing. 'But when I'm in the obsessive stage, I'm a sponge. I'm not a whole lot of use to anybody. Wherever I am, obviously that's where the physical part of me inhabits space.' But always a large part of his mind is back at the typewriter 'staring at white paper, wondering how in hell to fill it with words'.

Both Nimoy and Goldman recognise the importance of exercising their mental muscles wherever and whenever the opportunity arises, as well as turning ordinary experiences into work-outs for their minds. You can cultivate this quality in yourself by following Nimoy's advice and becoming interested in a wide range of projects and ideas. It doesn't matter whether they are personal, political, environmental, hobby activities or business-related as long as they are sufficiently varied and stimulating to provide plenty of raw materials for your idea factory.

Literary lightning rods

Writer Marshall Cook talks about creating a 'literary lightning rod' to draw inspiration to you whenever you need it. He sees this as teaching your creative right brain to work in harmony with its more orderly mental partner, the critical left brain.

He advocates a seven-step process:

1 *Feed the muse*
   Provide plenty of raw materials for your idea factory, using the tools described in this chapter.

2 *Nurture the idea*
   You can do this using the UFOS method previously described. Remember, this stands for Unlimited, Flexible, Original and Specific.

3 *Ignore the idea until it demands your fullest attention*
   This happens when your subconscious—your idea factory—has had plenty of time to mull the idea over. This period is sometimes called the incubation stage.

4 *Welcome the idea back*
   You do this by devoting your most productive writing time and energy to the task.

5 *Develop and write the idea*
   This should be in draft form with no consideration for 'manner' or style, only for content. As Cook points out, you can revise for clarity and coherence later, but you can't breathe life into a stillborn manuscript.

6 *Sustain the flow*
   Cook suggests always leaving off at a point where you know what will come next. Hemingway swore by the rule and it worked for him. There is a tendency to go on writing to the end of a paragraph or chapter, but it is easier to pick up where you left off if your direction is already set. Leaving a half-finished sentence with some notes on the direction of the rest may be enough to get you writing again when you come back to it.

7 *Revise and polish the work*
   This is the left-brain stage which Hemingway defined as 'trying to get the words right'. It helps to allow time

Finish writing when you
know what comes next.

between writing and editing so you become objective about the work, seeing both its virtues and its flaws so you can more closely shape it to your vision and ensure it communicates your intentions accurately.

Skills to cultivate

Creative people have a number of skills in common. Cultivating them provides a mental climate in which ideas can take root and grow. These skills are:

- ability to define the problem or the result required
- ability to see different points of view
- willingness to keep an open mind, not prejudging
- understanding how different elements might be combined
- sense of humour

133

- ability to visualise and fantasise
- ability to play

Some of these were explored in earlier chapters. Later we'll look at the roles of fantasy and visualisation in idea generation. When all these qualities are combined, you can make maximum use of the 'tools of the idea trade' such as brainstorming, clustering, daydreaming and journal keeping.

Brainstorming

This process was invented in 1941 by Dr Alex Osborn of the Creative Education Foundation of America. He called it 'organised ideation . . . a method by which we can use our brains to storm creative problems in a way that keeps judgment from jamming imagination'. The process is now used by large companies all over the world as well as by governments and individuals in all walks of life.

According to Robert J. O'Reilly in *Dynamic Thinking*, the great strength of this technique is that it 'picks conventional thinking up by the scruff of the neck and shakes it'. It gives your creative right brain a chance to have its say, free of the restrictions of your editing left brain.

The ground rules are simple. You start by posing a problem for which you require a creative solution. It may be the need for a book title, the need for a new word such as David Gerrold's name for his fuzzy creatures, or a logistics problem such as finding enough time in a busy day in which to write.

Whatever the problem, you should spell it out as succinctly as possible. Remember to focus on the result you seek:

134

I need to find an hour a day in which to write.
I need a title for my science fiction story.
I need a name for my fuzzy creatures.

At the outset, no criticism or evaluation is allowed. This rules out comments such as 'We've tried that and it didn't work' or 'We already have that on the list.' It also means no comments of a positive nature either. The habit of judging ideas as they arise is so strong that you'll be sorely tempted to say things like 'Hey, that's a good idea' or 'That would take more money than we have' and so on.

Any kind of value judgment, even of a positive nature, signals a shift out of the creative right brain and into the critical left brain and immediately applies the mental brakes to your thinking. In brainstorming you want to generate as many ideas as you can, the wilder the better. There will be ample time later to tame them.

You must also ask yourself whether those wild ideas are really as wild as they seem. As psychologist Denis Waitley observes: One of the Apollo astronauts had an inspiration for what became his life's work on the way back from the moon. Which is easier to accept—that he had a flash of inspiration or that he had it on the way back from the moon? Ideas which seem wild today may well seem commonplace tomorrow, if they even take that long. Consider the 'miracle' of microwave cooking, cellular telephones, computers with CD-ROM drives. All seemed to be wild ideas once upon a time.

Aim for quantity

During brainstorming the group should agree that quantity is the aim. Set a target of how many ideas you will generate in the time available. Don't stop until you've generated this number of possibilities or more.

In workshops we've brainstormed an age-old problem, that of finding time to write. How do you give yourself an hour a day in which to write? What might be your options? Some of the suggestions have included:

get up earlier
cut out lunch hour
stay up later at night
write during tea breaks
watch less television
ration conversation time
work four ten-hour workdays
don't get sidetracked with trivia
shop less often, buy more at a time
work while commuting
work in the bathtub
carry a dictaphone while doing other chores
use the time spent in queues or waiting on the phone
fool yourself—set the clock wrong
give up one meal a day
pay the kids to babysit each other
shower every second day
farm the kids out to neighbours after school
teach your partner to cook
stay an hour later at work and write there

As you can see, some of the suggestions are obvious; others are quite fanciful but contain the seeds of workable ideas. This is where you come to the fourth stage of the ISISI process. You've identified the problem—time in which to write; surveyed its world; used brainstorming as the ideation process.

136

Now you become selective, weeding out the impractical ideas and seeing whether the others can be combined, improved upon or have some aspect altered to achieve the result desired.

Working while commuting is a viable solution. I completed a four-year advertising diploma course in one year by studying during the 90-minute train journey to and from my job. Farming out the kids may seem impractical until you examine it more closely. If you know another writer who has children, can you take turns minding each other's children? Or get together with other parent-writers and form a playgroup where the children can play together while the adults do some creative work?

Staying late at the office may not only provide you with the quiet and focus needed for creative work but also gain you brownie points from your superiors, who aren't to know that your head-down devotion to duty isn't all that it appears. The possibilities of this idea are currently being explored by school teachers who are opening schools after hours so that students can do their 'homework' in a quiet environment more conducive to study than their homes.

Can you come up with alternatives which aren't on this list?

Brainstorming can also be done alone, on paper, but the benefits of working with a group include the high level of creative energy generated and the many different points of view which can be shared.

Clustering

Another kind of brainstorming, this time on paper, is clustering. It helps you to focus your thoughts and access different directions of thinking about a given subject. Proponents of clustering include the writers William Goldman and Irving Wallace. It works because it quiets the critical left side of the brain and encourages 'outside the boundaries' thinking, sometimes leading you to make connections you might otherwise have overlooked.

In *Writing the Natural Way*, Gabriele Lusser Rico suggests starting with a key word as a nucleus to evoke 'clusters' of associations. Spilling random words and phrases out around a centre creates a moment when you suddenly sense a focus for writing, says Rico. Applied to business-related or personal problems, the clustering process helps you to order your thoughts and gain new insights into the problem itself.

You begin clustering by writing a nucleus word in a circle in the centre of a blank page. Then you simply write down any connection which comes into your head. Write each word or phrase quickly with a line connecting it to the word in the circle, so your thoughts form a cluster around the main idea. Write in any direction you like around the central word, letting each thought feed off the last one until you exhaust that line of thought. If a new direction occurs to you, start a new radiant from the centre and follow this until you've exhausted it. Work as fast as you can and avoid censoring anything which comes to mind. Keep going until you can't think of another connection, or until you reach a breakthrough moment when you recognise a word or thought you can build on.

The writer and teacher Barry Watts uses clustering in his seminars on creative thinking. He encourages students to write fast, untidily and without analysing whatever comes out until every possible connection is exhausted. This enables you to stay in your creative right brain, only later turning the proceeds over to the left brain for analysis and development.

Barry calls the cluster a web and refers to the lines radiating out from the centre as stems, each of which more or less represents a line of thinking.

Since emotional and imaginative memories are stored in the right brain, clustering can be used to give you insights into your own emotional processes. However, this kind of clustering should only be attempted with the guidance of a trained counsellor. As Barry Watts points out, 'catacombs and dragons are in the right brain', frequently containing images and memories which your left brain has shielded you from for your own protection and peace of mind. You may not be emotionally ready to handle some of this material yet.

For this reason, you shouldn't put strictly negative or emotionally loaded words into the centre of the cluster—words such as drunkenness, fear, brutality, anger and so on—unless you have access to professional support to help you interpret and cope with the outcome.

Used intelligently and carefully, clustering is an excellent way to free your mind to make fascinating and sometimes totally unexpected connections.

The lonely creator

Try doing a clustering exercise with the word IDEAS in the centre of the blank page. As rapidly as you can, making no attempt at coherence or tidiness, spill out every word or phrase which comes to mind around the word IDEAS.

In the example given on p. 140, some of the connections are obvious, such as 'thinking' and 'special'. Less obvious but more interesting are words like 'isolation' and 'loneliness'. This exercise was done by a writer who was blocked on a writing project. Did she equate writing with the pain and

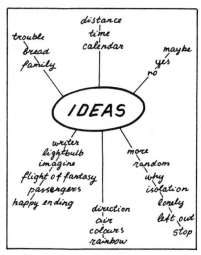

Clustering

isolation of a creative existence? Another of this writer's stems seems to follow a time-related theme, with words such as 'calendar' and 'distance'. The writer is a working journalist who, not surprisingly, equates ideas with deadlines.

Less predictable is the 'family' stem on the top left, which goes through 'sisters' and 'family' all the way to 'trouble'. Is creativity a burden for this writer? Knowing that her father left the family when the writer was a teenager, a connection could be made between the pressures and loneliness of a creative life, and the need to produce for the family's sake— the writer was the family breadwinner for a time.

The clusters you produce will not always be as transparent as this example. Sometimes you will be baffled by the connections your right brain makes out of a seemingly innocuous word. But pay careful attention to all the connections. They are telling you something about the direction and relationships your mind makes to this word or idea.

Labouring in the vignettes

Barry Watts suggests building on the cluster by turning one or more of the stems into a vignette, a little story linking the various images in the stem together. You do this by inserting as few connecting words as possible to form the stem into a coherent message or story. Start with the word which 'speaks' to you most strongly, one which may have triggered off many other associations. This may help you to turn the random thoughts in the cluster into a more recognisable pattern. For example, in the cluster shown, a vignette might be made from the stem starting with 'writer' and 'light bulb'. The sentence might read, 'A light bulb shone above the writer as he spun flights of fantasy, his readers passengers on a journey to a happy ending.'

Of itself this process may not start you writing in the direction you expected, but it may well trigger off other associations until before you know it, your thinking is focused and a story is taking shape.

Journals and notebooks

Another tool of the idea trade, the journal or notebook, has already been mentioned and many writers swear by them. Writing in a journal is stress-free and often enables you to switch more readily into right brain while keeping your writing muscle exercised at the same time.

If you get into the habit of writing in your journal at the same time and place each day, it will become as much a part of your routine as brushing your teeth. Writers who keep journals say they miss the work if for some reason they are unable to make an entry for a time.

What you write in your journal doesn't seem to matter as much as the act of writing itself. Random thoughts, stray ideas, snatches of overheard conversation, interesting words and descriptions, all can be scribbled down. Draw pictures if you like. Doodle. This is the kind of for-your-eyes-only work which may have no apparent benefit right away, but at the least will keep you in the habit of writing something every day.

The final tools of the idea trade are daydreams and visualisation, which are important enough to deserve a chapter to themselves. Combined with the previous tools, they provide almost all the resources your idea factory will ever need.

In a nutshell

1 Like a muscle, creative ability can be strengthened with practice.
2 Seek out and embrace change and novelty to boost your creativity.
3 Create a 'literary lightning rod' to draw inspiration to you using seven steps:
    - feed the muse
    - nurture the idea
    - ignore the idea
    - welcome the idea back
    - develop the idea
    - sustain the flow

- revise and polish
4 Creative people can:
  - define a problem
  - see different points of view
  - keep an open mind
  - see different combinations
  - visualise and fantasise
  - have a sense of humour
  - play
5 Creative tools which strengthen your mental muscles include:
  - brainstorming
  - clustering
  - journal or notebook keeping
  - daydreaming and visualisation

10

Daydream believers

'Art happens,' says Margaret Atwood. 'It happens when you have the craft and the vocation and are waiting for something else, something extra . . . It's the extra rabbit coming out of the hat, the one you didn't put there.' John Galsworthy called it 'quiet brooding' and considered it the most fruitful thing a writer could do.

So what is this 'quiet brooding' and how does it differ from idly staring out of a window?

In truth there's no difference. Staring out of a window is one of the best ways to quiet a busy mind and allow the accumulated material in your idea factory to wend its way to the surface in the form of an idea. It's the 'waiting' which Margaret Atwood advocates in order to make art 'happen'. Of course *you* put the extra rabbit into the hat. You just don't know it until you see it and a voice in your head says, 'Did I do that?' But the elements are stored away in your subconscious and the quiet brooding allows you to access them.

According to Henry Miller, most writing is done 'away from the typewriter, away from the desk . . . in the quiet, silent moments while you're walking or shaving or playing a game or even talking to someone you're not vitally interested in.'

This writing away from the typewriter is a vital part of the writer's craft but is much misunderstood, even by writers themselves. The problem is that nowadays doing nothing is regarded as a sign of laziness, of being unproductive. 'Looking busy' has been elevated to an art form in many organisations.

When I first started working at home I shared an office with my husband, a freelance cartoonist. We had to erect a partition between our desks so I could go on daydreaming without feeling as if I ought to be *doing* something. It wasn't outside criticism which bothered me, but the internal 'parent' telling me that daydreaming is a waste of time.

What's in a name?

If it helps, try giving your daydreaming a more respectable name. Conceptualising has a nice ring to it. Visualisation is another acceptable term for much the same activity. Call it mental imaging, reflection, whatever provides the freedom to give your brain the quiet moments in which to process the material you've acquired from various sources and combine it into new thoughts. You can't do this when your mind is busy and active. It's like trying to work a computer while the 'machine busy' signal is on. This tells you the computer is processing the previous set of instructions. If a machine is smart enough to know when it needs some quiet downtime, why not a writer?

Daydreaming can be one of the most productive ways to come up with new ideas and ways to solve problems. It's like having an imaginary TV screen inside your head. Only you can see the pictures being shown on it and you also have the power to move around and change the picture.

For example, picture your bedroom as you last saw it. Is the bed made or unmade? Are there clothes lying around or is everything neat and orderly? Is there a window? Is it covered or uncovered? Open or closed? What view can be seen from the window?

Now think of your dressing table or a chest of drawers on which you keep things like a brush and comb. When you last saw them, were they lying on top of the furniture or did you put them away? Are there any photographs in sight? Who is in them? What are the frames like?

This simple mental exercise requires you to take an imaginary TV camera into the room. When you pictured the whole room the camera was set to wide-angle and took in most of the furniture and furnishings. Then you had to move your mental camera over to the window to capture the view outside. Finally you needed to switch to a mental close-up lens to 'zoom in' on your dresser and see the comb, brush and any photographs there.

In writing you often have to decide what to describe in a scene and what to leave out. Doing a visualisation exercise like this one can answer the question easily. Let your mind be a camera again, this time roving around the imaginary scene in your story. Carrying the 'camera', your character enters the scene. Close your eyes. What does the character's camera focus on when they first enter the room?

The items which the camera notices most vividly are the ones to which you should restrict your description. Is there anyone else in the room when the character enters it? If so, what are they doing? How do they react to the character's entrance? If the room is empty at first, does anyone else come in after the character? What do they do? What does the character say in response?

Using your mental camera to photograph the scene will help you to visualise the scene and identify the elements which need to be included in your description.

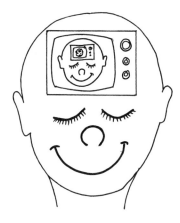

This can be done as an exercise in creative imagery or to help you solve a writing problem. In both cases it's a good idea to keep a notebook handy and write down your impressions as soon as you reopen your eyes.

Your private TV screen

Some writers say they always picture scenes as if they were being watched on an imaginary television screen. The writer acts like the producer of the program, scripting the scenes and movements as described above, then writes down what is seen and heard. Being aware that you can project whatever you like on your mental screen provides you with a powerful tool for bringing your writing to life.

This method forces you to write in scenes, much more vividly than you might otherwise do. You're also likely to find yourself cutting out a lot of extraneous description, zeroing in on the details which matter most instead. This is because you will be seeing the scene through the character's eyes rather than through the author's godlike perspective.

You can use daydreaming and visualisation to make the most of whichever relaxation exercises you use. In chakra meditation, for example, each of the energy fields on which you are asked to focus is identified with a different colour.

Close your eyes and imagine the colour *red*. Now bring to mind the image of a strawberry. Which was easier to picture? Most people agree it is the strawberry, because that is a concrete image, while a colour is an abstract. Associating each colour with a vivid image is a good way to bring the colours into your mind, such as the sky for blue, grass for green, an orange for orange and the sun for yellow.

Letting go

Daydreaming and visualisation are processes which can't be forced. You have to create the right mental framework and then *allow* them to occur. Just think of all the times you've gone to bed and tried to *will* yourself to fall asleep. It's late, you're tired. You have to be up early next morning, so sleep already! But it doesn't happen. The more you try to force yourself to sleep, the more wide awake you become.

It's usually only when you stop fighting yourself and occupy your mind with other things that sleep comes. There are many relaxation exercises you can use to occupy your mind, from the time-honoured one of counting sheep to deliberately relaxing every part of your body starting with your toes, knees, thighs and so on all the way to the top of your head. Most people fall asleep before they've completed the entire exercise because they've stopped fighting sleep and allowed it to come.

Dare to be idle

There seems to be a need for a period of quiet contemplation in order for ideas to reveal themselves to your conscious mind. Noted teacher of writing Brenda Ueland says, 'This quiet looking and thinking is the imagination, it is letting in ideas. Willing is doing something you have been told by someone else; there is no new imaginative understanding in it.'

'Dare to be idle' and the ideas will come, she says. However it is important to be idle in a constructive way. Being idle in front of an action-packed video is unlikely to generate ideas. Being idle over the latest thriller will also fill your mind when the very purpose of daydreaming is to empty your mind of day-to-day concerns so that you can have 'those new thoughts which nobody ever thought before'.

I find it helps to type my random thoughts onto paper. Anything will do. You can even spell out the problem on paper like so:

> I'm sitting here at the machine typing out my wish for an idea about what my character can do next. Let me see. I left the heroine in the arms of a man she thought loved her. Of course he didn't. What are they doing now that the hero has stormed off? What is he doing and thinking? Maybe I could . . .

After this comes a stream of possibilities which come faster and faster, the typing becoming less and less tidy as I explore what these people might do and say next.

Ask questions

Another useful way to develop a constructive daydreaming mood is to ask questions of your characters. Who are you? What do you want from life? What do you care about most? Hate the most? Then let the answers come to you in whatever form they choose without trying to force them or edit the results in any way.

At first the answers will probably come slowly, but if you stay with it they will gradually pick up speed until your pen can hardly keep pace. I learned this method from the late Gene Roddenberry, who used it to create the character of the logical pointed-eared Vulcan, Mr Spock. It wasn't metaphysical, Gene said, but merely a means of accessing information buried below conscious recall.

Writing teacher Barry Watts takes it a step further. He

says you can try writing your questions with your normal writing hand then switch the pen to your non-dominant hand to write the answers. This may feel awkward at first but may give you greater access to your creative right brain.

Exercises such as this one help to 'warm up' your writing muscle, much as you would warm up your car's engine before driving off on a cold morning. Even the term is appropriate—idling. You're letting your brain idle and warm up before going full throttle with whatever ideas come up.

'Begin with thyself,' said Marcus Aurelius, one of the 'five good emperors' of Rome. His reflections and insights are as relevant today as they were 120 years before Christ. 'Remember, that which pulls the strings is the thing which is hidden within.'

Visualisation

Being able to visualise helps you to solve problems and generate ideas because it puts you into a more relaxed frame of mind. You can also visualise scenes, look at them from different angles, rearrange them in your mind, in ways which might be impossible in the real world. Science fiction writers and historical writers use visualisation as a tool because they are largely unable to visit the scenes they write about.

To be able to visualise, you need to satisfy five conditions:

1   Quiet, peaceful surroundings. The fewer distractions you have, the more easily you will be able to conjure up pictures in your mind.
2   A quiet mind. You cannot visualise while thinking about a business deadline, dental appointment or what you might have for lunch. Choose a time when you have few

mental distractions and are unlikely to be interrupted for a time. Switch on the answering machine or take the phone off the hook.

3   A relaxed body. If you are tense and anxious your attention will be distracted by your bodily sensations. Ideally you should be able to 'let go' of your physical surroundings and retreat into your mind as if you were looking at a television screen inside your own head.

4   The ability to concentrate. If you have ever tried to fix your mind on one subject for a certain period, even as brief as a few minutes, you'll know how easily your thoughts wander. It takes practice to be able to keep your attention on one thought even for a few minutes. If you find it difficult, try closing your eyes and imagining a black velvet curtain being drawn across your thoughts. See only the curtain. When you're ready, superimpose what you want to focus on over the velvet curtain so you see only the object, nothing else. Examine it in minute detail. Turn it around the way a computer does a three-dimensional image. See it from all sides. Try to describe it in great detail in your mind. This helps to focus your concentration. Practice will further improve your ability.

5   The ability to *see* accurately. We've already examined how easy it is to look at something without really seeing it. Your watch is a typical example. You look at it dozens of times a day yet when it comes to describing it accurately most of us have surprising difficulty. The more you work at seeing things accurately, the easier it will be to bring detailed images to mind when you wish to use visualisation as a writing aid.

Visualisation is also a private experience. No-one can

share your mental images unless you describe them or write them down. This leaves you free to explore your mental images without fear of criticism.

When you have a problem to solve, creating a mental image of it and exploring it can help you come to grips with all its ramifications. Chess masters, for example, not only picture the board in their minds but can also visualise how it will look many moves ahead to anticipate the likely outcomes of an intended move. With practice, the ability to visualise can also help you to screen out distractions such as a busy office or home environment and allow you to write whenever you wish to.

Right brain or left brain?

The ability to visualise has long been thought of as a function of the creative right side of the brain, but researchers have begun to question this belief. While damage to the right side of the brain may impair spatial thinking, the injured person may still be able to construct mental images. So it seems more likely that the ability to visualise involves a group of functions located in different parts of the brain and called on in various combinations according to the task at hand.

There are several different types of visualisation: memory, imagination, daydreams and fantasies, illusions or visions.

Memory

As far as we know, the human memory works a bit like a library. In it we store short-term and long-term memories and impressions, although exactly how they are organised and encoded is still being researched. The stored impressions can be accessed when you visualise. For instance, in our earlier example you recalled what your bedroom looked like when you last saw it. You probably called to mind a mental picture of the room, trying to 'see' the details in your mind. It seems that memories are more accessible and clearer when the original information is clear at the time of storage. This is why writers should make the effort to really see the world rather than merely looking at it. The more details you store in your memory, the more accurate will be the images you are able to recall as prompts for your idea factory.

Don't just store away visual details. Try to soak up as many sensory impressions of an experience as you can, being aware that this is what you are doing. What does the experience sound like? Try to separate out as many individual sounds as you can so you are fully aware of them. Familiar smells are another powerful memory trigger. The scent of newly baked bread, freshly picked rosemary, hospital disinfectant and the like may be enough to trigger quite detailed associations from as far back as early childhood, so try to store these impressions as well.

The cognitive interview

A method called the cognitive interview has been devised by Edward Geiselmann and his colleagues at the University of California in Los Angeles. Designed to improve the accuracy of eyewitness testimony in solving crimes, it can also be used to improve your own recall of events as an aid to more vivid writing.

The system involves following a series of steps in a fixed order:

- Mentally relive (visualise) the environment and personal context which existed at the time of the event. Where were you? What were you doing? Were there others around you? What were they doing? What was the weather like? The temperature?
- Report everything, no matter how unimportant it might seem to be.
- Try reporting everything in a succession of different time sequences. Imagine it happened early in the morning, then at night.
- Report the event from a variety of different perspectives. If you were with a friend, try to imagine the event from the friend's point of view.

All of these steps will help you to bring the event or experience to mind in sufficient detail for you to be able to write about it more accurately and vividly.

Imagination

Before you can construct images in your mind, you need raw materials provided by your five senses—what you see, hear, taste, touch and smell. When you use imagination to construct mental images, you use bits and pieces of these memories and rearrange or alter them to create new images.

Think of an elephant driving a car. A tree with cotton wool instead of leaves. The sun with a smiling face. Again, the more impressions you have stored in memory, the more resources you will have to create imaginary mental images. In a later chapter we'll look at ways you can provide yourself with a greater variety of these mental 'raw materials'.

Daydreams and fantasies

These are a combination of memory and imagination. They may comprise past or projected (future) experiences. If you are planning to go on a holiday, you have probably pictured yourself in the holiday setting as you pored over the travel brochures. These sorts of daydreams and fantasies are so pleasant they can sometimes seem more vivid than the real world around you.

Visions

Finally there are illusions or visions, which an individual may confuse with reality. Other people are generally not able to share the visions, although to the person experiencing them they may seem startlingly real. Another fleeting kind of visualisation is the after-image which occurs after you stare at a bright light.

Since visions and after-images are not normally under your conscious control, they are not as useful as the other categories of visualisation in helping you to generate ideas. A combination of memory, imagination and fantasy can be a fertile source of raw material for your writing. By providing yourself with the conditions of a quiet mind and body, concentrating and simply allowing whatever comes into your mind, you can create the conditions under which ideas come surprisingly readily.

You can practise visualisation by setting yourself deliberate exercises. For example, what would an elephant look like driving a car? Close your eyes and try to conjure up a detailed picture of this or some other unusual subject. Imagine a person with whom you're having problems. In your mind, put this person into a cage in the zoo. Feel better now? Visualisation is a wonderful tool for developing ideas but it should also have that marvellous quality of *sanuk*!

In a nutshell

1   Daydreaming is an essential tool for idea generation. Call it conceptualising or mental imaging if it helps.
2   To decide what to include in a scene, have your character take a mental camera into the scene and then describe what the 'camera' sees.
3   Picture scenes in your mind as if seeing them on an imaginary TV screen.
4   Don't try to force images. Dare to be idle and allow them to come. Learning a relaxation or meditation technique helps.
5   Ask questions of your characters to bring them to life.
6   To visualise, you need: peaceful surroundings, a quiet mind, a relaxed body, the ability to concentrate, the ability to *see* accurately.
7   Visualisation includes memory, imagination, daydreams and fantasies, visions and after-images.

11

Write while you sleep

Sleep, which the poet William Wordsworth called 'the mother of fresh thoughts', can be one of the greatest incubators of new ideas—the night shift of your idea factory, if you like.

Dreams occur in the Rapid Eye Movement (REM) phase of sleep, when we see dreams as if they were being projected on the movie screen of our minds.

There are also the images which occur before we drift off to sleep (hypnagogic) and before we become fully awake (hypnopompic). These peculiar states of consciousness, when we are not quite awake and not quite asleep, can be rich sources of creative inspiration. The poet Samuel Taylor Coleridge and the scientist Albert Einstein are among the great thinkers who have said they produced some of their best ideas during these periods.

It is thought that the combination of physical and mental relaxation as well as freedom from distractions makes it easier to develop new frames of reference for problem solving and idea generation. In this dreamy state, similar to a hypnotic trance, the mind seems more able to accept suggestions and to perceive complex issues more clearly.

During hypnagogic and hypnopompic periods there are measurable changes in brainwave activity, and the brainwaves produced during these times are most closely associated with creativity and idea generation. As measured by an electroencephalograph (EEG), the four types of brainwave activity are as follows.

Alpha

The German psychiatrist Hans Berger names this rhythmical frequency alpha because it was the first to be observed on the EEG. Alpha waves range from eight to thirteen cycles per second and are now associated with calm, alert, pleasant, meditative experiences. Generally, this state is considered to be the borderline between conscious and unconscious mental activity. Alpha waves were first observed in the part of the brain associated with vision, but have since been observed at other cerebral sites as well.

Beta

Ranging from thirteen cycles per second on the EEG to as high as forty or fifty under stress, these are the fast, low-voltage brainwaves commonly associated with conscious activity and problem solving. Beta waves are the most commonly measured brainwaves and their presence is reflected in the 'aware' usage of the five senses.

Delta

After some time in the alpha state, the brainwaves slow to delta frequency—around four cycles per second. These slower, high-voltage brainwaves are associated with a profound trancelike state and are usually only observable during deep sleep.

Theta

At four to seven cycles per second, these brainwaves are usually associated with the drowsy 'reverie' or 'illumination' state, when creative imagery tends to appear. Theta waves are often found mingled with alpha waves, which are also associated with creative activity and dreams.

Alpha and theta, the slower brainwave cycles, seem to occur when the gap is narrowed between the conscious and unconscious states. In order to be aware of the imagery associated with theta waves during the drowsy states, we may also need to produce some alpha waves to provide a sort of conscious 'carrier wave'.

Whether it is called hypnagogia, daydreaming or Galsworthy's 'quiet brooding', in the alpha–theta state it is easier for the mind to form new connections, think of new metaphors and work within new frames of reference than can be done when we produce the beta brainwaves of conscious reasoning.

Thomas Edison supposedly conceived many of his inventions in the drowsy state preceding the many catnaps he was known to enjoy. Writer Robert Louis Stevenson used his dream states to produce some of his most famous stories, including *Dr Jekyll and Mr Hyde*. Elias Howe and his sewing machine needle is another well-known example of a workable solution being derived during a dream state.

Experiments with the EEG and other measuring devices have shown that with practice, individuals can produce different brainwave combinations. Through a combination of mental and physical relaxation, you can learn to produce the alpha and theta waves most associated with creativity.

Small biofeedback monitors can be purchased from electrical stores and used at home to monitor changes in hand temperature and muscle tension associated with a change in the brainwaves being produced. I use one such device, which makes a high-pitched sound that gradually slows to a tock-tock-tock when relaxation is achieved. People using some such device are more easily able to produce the alpha and theta brainwaves, but you can achieve a similar state without a monitor through relaxation and meditation exercises.

The importance of relaxation

Watch any child writing and see how tightly she grips the pencil. Her tongue probably protrudes from between clenched teeth and she is unaware of the world around her as she concentrates.

When you learn how to do anything, you start by giving it your conscious attention, like the child learning to write. Once learned, the knowledge is stored in your subconscious mind. Now, whenever you want to write something down, you have only to think about what you want to write, not about the act of writing itself.

The same applies to learning to access the alpha–theta state. First you use your conscious mind to practise physical and mental relaxation until it becomes as routine as the physical act of writing. Like acquiring any habit, it takes practice and a willingness to commit a regular amount of time each day. I try to do a relaxation exercise for 30 minutes on at least five days out of seven. The more you do it the easier it gets, but you should allow at least 30 days before it becomes a habit. There are many relaxation guides and tapes available,

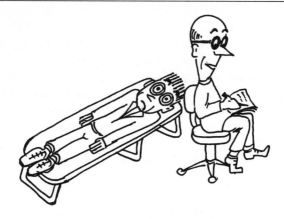

"I don't think you're relaxed enough yet."

so experiment with several types until you find the one that suits you best.

If you're not used to concentrating, you can try the exercise described previously, of drawing a black velvet curtain across your thoughts. On the curtain put your favourite flower. See it in great detail as if it were indeed fixed to the front of the curtain. Then let it gradually fade from sight until all you're left with is the rich, deep black velvet of the curtain.

Even if you can only picture the flower and the black curtain for a few seconds at a time, you can be fairly sure that for those few seconds you were in the alpha–theta state. The more you practise quieting your mind, the easier it will become.

A few people find they are unable to get any sort of mental picture at all. It may be that you're expecting too much. What appears on the 'screen of the mind' is seldom

162

as clear or vivid as the images on a television screen or in a magazine. Be content with any image you are able to create in your mind, or even a field of grey or black mist if this is easier for you to picture.

If you find the closed-eyed meditations too difficult to achieve or your mind keeps wandering, there is an open-eyed version you can try. It is both calming and refreshing and can be done with almost any handy object—a piece of fruit, a picture or any small object that is pleasing and interesting to look upon.

Place the object on a cleared space in front of you on a desk or table. Now sit comfortably and, relaxing your eyes, gaze steadily at the object. Keep your eyes relaxed so you look with interest rather than staring fixedly. Try to see every detail of the object's surface. Let your thoughts explore what might be inside. Think about where the object came from, its purpose and how it was made. Channel all your thoughts steadily into the object, pushing away any other thoughts that try to intrude into your mind.

This exercise helps to straighten out the jumble of impressions usually crowding your mind. After a few minutes you should feel tranquil and relaxed. If you have access to a biofeedback monitor you should find you are well into the alpha–theta state.

Problem solving

When you have achieved a tranquil mental state and are able to sustain it for however brief a time, you can try using it to help you solve creative problems or supply you with ideas you need for your writing.

163

In *The Intuitive Edge*, Philip Goldberg suggests dropping a problem, question or dilemma into your mind like a letter into a mailbox. 'A hazy thought, the merest idea, will be better than a precise verbal statement. Drop it in and let it go.' Have a notebook or tape recorder near to hand and grab it before you do anything else immediately after your meditative period. You'll be surprised at what appears, says Goldberg.

There are four main reasons why we are most creative and open to new ideas during sleep or when we produce alpha–theta brainwaves (hypnagogic and hypnopompic periods). They are as follows.

Refreshment

Rest, whether physical or mental, is a prerequisite for fresh thought. This is why you so often gain new insights when you walk away from a project for a while, or do something unrelated such as washing dishes or mowing the lawn. 'Sleeping on it' is frequently the best way to solve a problem—literally.

Anxiety reduction

When the nervous system is highly aroused you produce beta waves, the brainwaves of conscious reasoning. You become more anxious because the answer you seek won't come as easily as you'd like, and this causes more stress. Being able to relax reduces stress and makes it easier to access the creative alpha–theta state.

Creative freedom

Just as the sequence trap can prevent you from seeing alternative solutions and options, orderly daytime thought patterns

164

can prevent you from making creative leaps. You get into a kind of mental rut. During rest the mind is free to consider new possibilities, combinations and metaphors.

Information processing

When you're looking for a new idea you don't always look in all the possible places. Just as when I got hung up on speaker shelves instead of 'things to hold up speakers', the mind can selectively ignore information which doesn't fit a preconceived notion. During rest, information you may not be aware of having gathered can become available to you, or you might pay more attention to it than you would in full, alert consciousness. Your mind is also more inclined to experiment with new combinations of thoughts that you might resist during wakefulness. This is known as *sleep synthesis*.

Capture the lightning

Mozart wrote that his ideas flowed best and most abundantly when he was 'entirely alone and of good cheer'. He might be travelling in a carriage, walking after a good meal or lying awake at night. Possibly he was in a hypnagogic or hypnopompic state without having the words to identify it as such.

'Whence and how [ideas] come, I know not; nor can I force them,' he wrote. This emphasises the desirability of *allowing* the creative problem to solve itself rather than consciously trying to force an answer. Before you go to sleep at night, let your mind drift over the problem or the idea you need, then dismiss it from your thoughts.

When you plant a seed in this way, your mind keeps working on it while you sleep. It may be a day or more before the answer comes, and it may not come in the form you expect. But if you are open and receptive to whatever comes up, the answer will surely present itself.

Get into the habit of paying attention to any thoughts and ideas that come to you in the periods immediately before and after sleep. Keep a notebook or tape recorder by your bedside so you can capture these fleeting thoughts before they slip from your conscious grasp. My experience suggests that ideas arising during these periods are very easily lost. Next day you will probably recall that you had a good idea but you won't be able to remember what it was.

In a nutshell

1   The periods just before sleep (hypnagogic) and just after waking (hypnopompic) are rich sources of creative inspiration.

2   Of the four types of measurable brainwaves—alpha, beta, delta and theta—the alpha–theta mix is most associated with creativity.

3   Teach yourself to produce alpha–theta brainwaves by using a biofeedback monitor or by learning and practising a relaxation technique.

4   The main benefits of these states are refreshment, anxiety reduction, creative freedom and better information processing.

5   Keeping a notebook or tape recorder by your bedside allows you to capture ideas and impressions gained during the drowsy state.

12

The incubation process

As with using a computer, the productivity of your idea factory will depend on the quality of the raw materials you feed into it. Remember garbage in, garbage out?

Actor Leonard Nimoy calls these fresh resources the *goodies box*, after a comment made by Katharine Hepburn when she was being interviewed once on American television:

> You come into town with your box of goodies and that box of goodies is you, and you start to use it and sell it and eventually the box of goodies gets used up, and then you must go back to something else to fill up the box with some new goodies.

So where do you go to find these 'new goodies'? For me the ultimate irony is the writer who only writes about writers. This tells me more surely than anything else that the writer's goodies box is depleted. You can't replenish that box by spending all your time around other writers in a writer-oriented world.

The solution is to follow William Goldman's lead and turn yourself into a sponge. Soak up all the input you can from as many sources as possible. At the very least it will give you something new to write about and may well spark off ideas in entirely unexpected directions.

In *The Intuitive Edge*, Philip Goldberg christens this soaking up of experiences *absorption trips*, which he says you use to gather *soft data*. The hard data are the facts and figures you collect during research; the who, what, when, where and how of journalism. Soft data are harder to define and include all the sensory impressions of smells, shapes, colours and even illusions gathered on your absorption trips.

By illusions I mean things which exist only in the writer's imagination. These are the phantom characters you imagine inhabiting a real setting—the innocent paper seller your mind turns into a go-between for the underworld. This is the what-if element at work. You look at the world and see not only what *is* but what might be. You add two and two and get six.

Drawing from life

You can turn almost any aspect of your life into an absorption session. A visit to the dentist—what if he's making a fortune through illegally plundered gold teeth, or planting listening devices in the teeth of government officials? Grocery shopping—what if the seemingly innocent mother with her children is planting poison in everyday food items to make a political statement? Your speculations need have no bearing on what's really happening, or at least one would hope not. But this kind of thinking may explain why some writers report being contacted by law enforcement agencies who suspect them of knowing more than they reasonably should. It's really no more than a vivid imagination at work and the sense of being alert to possibilities as well as realities.

Make the most of opportunities as they present themselves. When visiting new towns or cities, explore the local businesses, talk to local people and find out all you can about what they do and how and, most importantly, why.

Talking to a stranger at a literary lunch for the writer Wilbur Smith resulted in my book *Love Like Gold*. I gained yet another plot idea from reading a newspaper story about a foundling who had been left in someone's garage. In most such cases the baby is soon identified, but I started to wonder what happens if it isn't? How would it feel to grow up without the slightest clue as to your origins? Wouldn't it affect your attitude toward love and marriage? You could be unwittingly passing on some genetic problem or marrying a close relative. From these speculations came *Man Without a Past*.

Idea triggers

Pinnacle romance author Ginna Gray says, 'It's really peculiar the things that trigger an idea in a writer's brain. A casual remark, an observation, a sound, a colour, a certain evocative smell . . . all set off a chain of memories and imagining, feelings of *déjà vu* or bubbly anticipation.'

Flora Speer says her ideas 'just come', although there is often a link between the subject matter she is researching for one book and the idea for the next. Research for a Viking romance turned up information about the Scottish king Macbeth which resulted in her first published book, *By Honour Bound*. At other times, Speer says, the idea comes as a flash of inspiration. At the theatre one night she was watching an actor in a white suit walk from shadow into spotlight. She visualised a knight in shining armour riding out of the rain into brilliant sunshine, and this became the inspiration for a two-volume family saga.

A third book was inspired by the play she was watching at the time, Shakespeare's *Much Ado About Nothing*.

Speer also remembers discussing with her father his work in the early space program. These discussions sparked an interest in space travel, the activities of NASA and astronomy, and eventually led to the development of a futuristic novel which combined her interests.

Going to the theatre, discussing her father's work in the space program, and reading Shakespeare are all absorption trips of one kind or another, opening the author to input from a wide variety of sources.

Invest yourself

William Goldman says that when he's not writing he sees and hears all sorts of things and consciously thinks, 'I ought to remember that, that may come in handy sometime.' Henry Miller also recognised that he was working when he was walking, shaving, playing a game or having a conversation. He called it 'writing away from the typewriter'.

Since it's almost impossible to predict which stimuli will result in a viable idea for a story or a book, it makes sense to provide yourself with as much raw material as you can from as many sources as possible.

There's an old joke about a man who pleaded daily with God to let him win the lottery. Time after time the lottery was drawn and the poor man won nothing, although he kept up his prayers. Finally, in desperation, God said to him, 'Help me out here, son. At least buy a ticket.' If you want to achieve a result you have to be prepared to invest yourself in your writing.

If you're working on a non-fiction project you can look up books and articles on related subjects, even if they aren't precisely concerned with the topic at hand. Research has shown that you can learn more easily about a given topic if you have already acquired some background information. Even if your study sources aren't directly related to your subject you can increase your memory potential by learning in adjacent areas. The proof of this is in the fact that you can learn a new language more easily once you have already mastered another foreign language.

Business executives use absorption sessions to manage their companies more effectively. It's called 'managing by wandering around' and gives the executive a feel for the company at all levels. The kinds of absorption trips involved here include serving behind counters, eating in staff canteens and chatting with workers during their breaks, and dealing with routine mail.

You can apply the same principles by visiting parts of your city to which you don't normally go, or call on different departments or branches of your employer. Regularly go to new clubs or restaurants other than those you habitually attend.

Take along a notepad or tape recorder on these absorption trips, not to record facts or to make sense of what you see, but to capture any interesting ideas that may arise out of the experience.

Follow your impulses. Don't plan where you'll go or what you'll see. Be open and allow the experience to guide you rather than the other way around.

Be open to new input

How often have you purchased a book on impulse, then found it contained exactly some bit of information you needed? On some unexplainable level, this seems to happen when you're open to receiving the information. It may simply be that your interest in a subject makes you more aware of related material but it is definitely part of the creative process.

Read all about it

The best-selling novelist Dean Koontz once said in an interview that he advised would-be writers to do two things. 'The first is to write, write, write. Concentrate on being a storyteller and develop your craft to the highest calibre possible.

'The second thing is to read, read, read. Read widely and extensively, in all areas. It doesn't matter what . . . you write, or wish to write . . . The more you broaden your interests as a reader, the more you will simultaneously broaden your perspective and your talent as a writer.

'When you first read a book, read it through the first time as a reader . . . When you have finished . . . analyse it . . . Try to discover the technique, the nuts and bolts with which the story was built. It may be hard at first but by simply making the effort . . . your subconscious will be absorbing vital information. And because your subconscious never sleeps, eventually it will make all sorts of associations and connections, and over time it will give you the critical understanding you are seeking.'

One of my favourite ways to absorb new material is through buying and reading magazines on many different subjects. My library includes magazines on everything from mountain climbing and goat breeding to farm management, pop music and space flight. None of these, except possibly space flight, is an interest of mine. In fact I bought the magazines *because* the subjects were new to me.

Have you ever gone to a newsagent and found they had sold out of your favourite daily paper? Or bought the local newspaper on a trip interstate or overseas? For most people this experience is mildly uncomfortable.

Most of us are comfortable with sameness, with reading the same opinion columns and comic strips and choosing television programs from the same guides or looking for sports results on the same pages. Adjusting to a different format, even when it contains much of the same information, creates mild discomfort. This is precisely why you should expose yourself to the experience deliberately.

Just as saturation can blind you to what your eyes actually see, familiarity can blunt your perceptions. Supermarket managers know this and frequently change their stock around so you are exposed to the full range of what they have to offer. Reading something as innocuous as a TV guide in a different format might alert you to channels other than those you customarily watch. In the habit of reading the same columns each day, you might overlook programs on, say, a foreign-language channel.

Reading magazines and books on subjects outside your areas of interest and expertise will also widen your mental horizons. I have no background or interest in farm management but bought a magazine on the subject purely for the information. Much of it read almost like a foreign language to me because specialist publications tend to speak the language of their readership, but it was also educational. People on the land have different concerns and even a slightly different language from city-dwellers. Should I have the need to create country-born characters, I now have a better chance of making them sound authentic.

You might also pick up some wonderful story ideas, as I did. Reading an issue of a farming journal led to my book *Man Shy*. The magazine featured a story about a young woman who served as a farm secretary and rotated her services among several properties as she organised their administration. I wrote to the young woman care of one of the properties and was rewarded with pages of fascinating and detailed information about her life and work. While the character I created was purely fictitious, the occupation was based on reality and so rang totally true.

Although I have lived in rural Australia and visited sheep stations and other properties, I had no idea that the occupation of farm secretary existed. It made a pleasant change. Previously my heroines were nannies, jillaroos or had other jobs limited by my own knowledge. Reading a few farm journals could change your thinking as it did mine.

A magazine on business travel provided more good background for another book, *That Midas Man*. Several scenes take place in an executive helicopter, the same one I rode in after reading about it in the magazine and contacting the Australian agents, who were delighted to help me. Specific details may not make or break a story, but they do add authenticity.

Ask and receive

By all rights, writers should be the most popular people at social gatherings. In the book *How to Win Friends and Influence People*, Dale Carnegie basically advises you to spend more time being interested in the other person than in the impact you are having. As well as making sound social sense (although I do wonder what happens if two people try to practise this suggestion on each other), it makes sense for your idea factory as well.

A writer should always be asking questions out of genuine interest. Asking questions not only flatters the other person, it provides plenty of grist for your idea mill. What kind of work do you do? Why did you choose this work? What is your typical day like? These are the kinds of questions whose answers will provide enough raw material to inspire dozens of stories.

The heroine of my book *A Fair Exchange* came out of one such experience. At an aerobics class I noticed a woman wearing a sweatshirt with an unfamiliar logo on it. It turned out to signify the International Agricultural Exchange Association. This group coordinates the activities of thousands of farm workers from dozens of countries who wish to work on farms in other countries around the world. At any one time there are hundreds of exchange workers living on farms, including in Australia.

You've never heard of them? Neither had I, but by the time Anne, the owner of the sweater, had explained the scheme to me, my writing antenna was positively quivering.

With her permission I interviewed her at her office and also spoke to participants in the scheme. I still think there's enormous scope for a non-fiction book on the subject, if anybody's interested.

Asking questions works, but it takes practice and genuine interest so you don't appear intrusive. The ability to interview people is a skill every writer should master, not only those interested in journalism. You don't want to be like the writer who interviewed the musician Dave Brubeck at Sydney airport. The writer's first question was supposedly, 'How many are in your quartet, Mr Brubeck?'

The why questions

In your interviews you should aim to obtain insights rather than hard information. The question asked of Dave Brubeck may be apocryphal, but it demonstrates the futility of using an interview to establish facts that can normally be obtained elsewhere.

What a writer should seek are insights and philosophies, answers to the 'why' questions, which are harder to find through factual research.

To get people to talk to you, it's usually enough to introduce yourself as a writer seeking information for an article or book. I have never yet been asked to prove my bona fides, although my name is far from being a household word.

It helps to come up with provocative and interesting questions which your subjects will enjoy answering. The American writer Joseph Bell kept Rex Harrison talking well beyond his allotted interview time by asking about Harrison's experiences working with Bernard Shaw. No other interviewer had mentioned it until Bell's research revealed the connection.

Interview subjects need not be famous to provide you with fascinating material. Some of my best input has come from people who have never been interviewed before, like the farm secretary and the organiser of the agricultural exchange program.

When interviewing someone by mail, make it as easy as possible for them. Set out clear, open-ended questions which don't require an essay to answer. I find it's fruitful to ask someone about a typical day. Of course you would always include return postage and a self-addressed envelope.

Finding interview subjects is easy. Keep your eyes and ears open at every gathering. Remember what the researcher Hugh Mackay points out—that you have two ears and one mouth, which should be used in those proportions. Having some business cards printed that you can leave with your subject will remind them of your name and purpose if you need to get in touch later.

Finger walking

Never underestimate the telephone book as a source of soft data. It's my favourite reference work and has seldom let me down. When I was writing a how-to book on plumbing repairs I desperately needed information on septic tanks. The phone book carried such a listing and I found a company from which I obtained all the information I needed. I think I was the first writer who'd ever contacted them.

When the interview was over the representative offered to send me samples of his company's products, which was a bit of a worry until I found out that they also made organic beauty products.

Off the record . . . some of the most interesting material can be obtained after you close your notebook. This doesn't mean that the interview is over, although many people mistakenly assume that it is. It's not unethical to use material gained after you've stopped taking notes unless you agree that what is said is 'off the record', when it must not be used at all.

The relaxed mood at the (apparent) end of an interview often produces some interesting and revealing insights. For this reason you should be careful what you say at this point if you are the interview subject. It's wise to consider that everything you say 'can and will be used in evidence' whether it seems to be part of the interview or not. If you don't want it quoted back at you, don't say it at all.

The French playwright Eugene Ionesco had the right idea when he asked, 'Why do people always expect authors to answer questions? I am an author because I want to *ask* questions. If I had answers I'd be a politician.'

Let ideas ferment

The very best wines are made by allowing the grapes to ferment for anything from a few days to several weeks. This turns the simple sugars fructose and glucose in the grapes into alcohol. In Germany the classic Rhine wines such as the Heidelberg Tun were formerly matured in huge casks for many years. Even today three years is the average.

While I don't suggest you should let your ideas ferment for as long as three years, you should get into the habit of letting them mature for as long as possible before you develop them. This gives you the objectivity to judge the ideas more honestly and dispassionately.

The best-selling novelist Colleen McCullough told members of the Society of Women Writers that she can't write about a subject while she is still 'too close' to it. *The Thorn Birds* wasn't written until Colleen had lived away from Australia for long enough to be objective about the subject matter.

This process can happen whether you intend it to or not. Some years ago I travelled by ship from Cairns to Cape York and Thursday Island, having planned the trip as a holiday. With no intention of writing about the experience, I didn't take notes, although I did collect background material. But primarily I saw the trip as a relaxing, enjoyable holiday. It was two years later before I was sufficiently distanced from the experience to start to see story possibilities in it. Soon afterwards my book *Island of Dreams* was condensed in *Woman's Day* magazine and then published as a novel worldwide.

Although it was one of the most ambitious absorption sessions I've undertaken, I didn't even know I was taking it at the time. Having learned from it, I now assume that every experience will find its way into a book sooner or later, probably later, when, like Colleen McCullough, I can be objective about it.

Avoid the rush

When an idea strikes, whether from one of your absorption sessions or from speculative reading or socialising, there's a temptation to try and capture it on paper right away, as if it could somehow escape otherwise.

It's far better to simply make a few notes about the idea and then file it away so that, like wine, it can ferment in its own juices. Just as drinking wine too early can spoil the experience, trying to develop an idea too quickly can rob it of its full potential.

Naturally not every idea will turn into a vintage story, any more than all wines become vintage drops. A process similar to wine-making also results in vinegar!

Only time will reveal whether your idea is a vintage one or not. Time and patience will also give you the ability to consider the idea from all sides, to develop it as fully as possible and to maximise its story potential.

Your treasure file

In *Overcoming Writing Blocks*, Kevin Mack and Eric Skjei recommend starting a treasure file of all the intriguing concepts and material which come your way. They suggest keeping the material in anything from a series of manila folders to a shoebox, or on index cards. To your own notes you can add newspaper clippings, cartoons, advertisements, letters, memos and anything else likely to be inspirational for your writing. The file works both as a starting point for fresh ideas when you run out and also as a reminder of 'abundance in the midst of an internal drought'.

Into the treasure file can also go the chunks of writing you're forced to delete during the editing process. Knowing you have somewhere to keep these chunks takes some of the pain out of the revisions. If you change your mind, the deletions can be rescued and reinstated or saved for use in another piece of work. Many computer programs have provisions for saving deleted copy in the electronic equivalent of the treasure file.

Just as Len Deighton saved his early drafts on a shelf because he couldn't bear to discard them, you can save whatever you wish in your treasure box. In future months, when the deleted items feel less like parts of yourself, you may feel more ready to discard them.

Sometimes an idea will turn out to be too slight on its own to make the basis of a story. However, combined with another idea, it might give you a strong plot. Some time ago I filed away a newspaper clipping about a photographic studio where seriously ill teenagers were helped through make-up and glamour photography to rediscover the beauty their illnesses had taken from them. The story brought a lump to my throat and I knew it had the makings of a plot, but at that point it was too 'thin' to be of real use so I let it sit and ferment.

Later I began toying with the idea of writing a modern fairytale about a contemporary prince and a reluctant Cinderella. Combined with the make-over story, I had the plot of my book *A Royal Romance*.

Stranger than fiction

The role of ideas in creativity is often misunderstood. Quite a few writers believe that it is somehow better to base a story on something which actually happened than to invent a plot.

Your absorption sessions are meant to provide you with raw material, not the stories themselves. These come from your own imagination and inventiveness, in the same way as the tapestry maker buys a canvas and a supply of wool and then weaves the two into a beautiful tapestry. The experiences

181

and input from your absorption sessions are the canvas and wool for your tapestry. Your writing skill is what weaves them into a convincing and entertaining story.

Just because a story is told exactly as it happened does not mean your readers will find it entertaining or even believable. Truth really is stranger than fiction. Many things that happen in real life are simply too unlikely to make convincing fiction, no matter how much you argue that they really happened.

It's the author's job to convince the reader. You are the salesperson and your story is your stock-in-trade. In workshops we do an exercise called 'What I meant was . . .' It involves having a volunteer describe to the audience a selection of geometric shapes which are drawn on a card visible only to the volunteer. The group members have to draw the shapes according to the verbal directions given. The volunteer can't use gestures or provide any information other than in words, because a writer can't gesture to a reader or fill in gaps with additional explanation. It's an extraordinarily difficult exercise both for the volunteer and for the group, but it does emphasise the point that a writer must include in a story everything the reader needs for full comprehension.

If the reader misses part of your message or finds it unconvincing, then further editing is needed, no matter how well you think you've made the point or how faithfully you've recounted the original experience. As Harlequin editor, Elizabeth Johnson, wisely pointed out to me, 'If I've missed it, bear in mind the readers will, too.'

Cosmic currents

Henry Miller described the most successful writers and artists as people who 'know how to hook up to the currents which are in the atmosphere, in the cosmos'. Great novels, great poems or any works of art are in the air, according to Miller, needing the artist as interpreter to capture them and bring them forth.

'Who is original?' Miller asks. 'Everything that we are doing, everything that we think, exists already, and we are only intermediaries . . . who make use of what is in the air.'

But first you need what Miller calls 'antennae' and a willingness to go out and 'hook up' to those creative currents. Or as Goldman puts it, be a sponge soaking up all that the world has to offer. This readiness more than almost anything else will help you to answer the question, 'Where do you get your ideas?'

The answer, as you now know, is 'everywhere'.

In a nutshell

1 Your idea factory needs lots of input to fill your 'goodies box' with raw material for ideas. Soak up as much material as you can from 'absorption trips' of all kinds.
2 Be alert for idea triggers when talking to strangers, visiting, shopping, or anywhere you happen to be.
3 Invest in your writing by reading widely, especially outside your normal areas of interest.
4 Listen more than you talk.
5 Develop your interviewing skills to obtain insights and philosophies not easily found through research.
6 Let your ideas ferment like good wine. Don't rush to capture them on paper too quickly.
7 Keep a treasure file of snippets and deleted copy for possible later use.

13

Eureka moments on demand

There's a good reason why scientists describe the best source of inspiration as 'the three Bs—bed, bath and bus'. Since your idea factory never stops working, it is often pursuing the solutions to your writing problems or turning the fruits of your absorption trips into plots while your left brain is occupied with mundane activities like bus travel or even while it is asleep.

To the three Bs I would add a fourth—box, as in television. Some of my best Eureka moments seem to come while I'm watching television late in the evening. Very few programs demand full attention so I find I can quite easily rough out some plot notes or draft letters while keeping one eye on the box. The program may well keep my left brain sufficiently distracted that my right brain is freed up for creative work.

Intuitive flashes

So what exactly is a Eureka moment? How do you recognise them, and more importantly, how can you encourage them to strike more often?

Tradition attributes the first Eureka moment to the Greek mathematician, physicist and inventor Archimedes. He supposedly discovered Archimedes' principle when he was asked by the king to determine whether a certain crown was made of pure gold or alloyed with silver. Archimedes was perplexed until one day, observing the overflow of water as he stepped into a public bath, he suddenly realised that gold and silver, being of different density, would displace different weights of water and that by means of this fact he could test the crown. Delighted at this discovery, he ran home without his clothes, shouting 'Eureka,' which means 'I have found it.'

Many of the great scientific and artistic discoveries are attributed to similar intuitive 'flashes'. Johann Gutenberg was drinking a glass of wine when it came to him that the same press which produced wine from grapes could be combined with a coin punch which imprinted a raised design on a coin surface, and printing was born.

Richard Wagner daydreamed of sinking into flowing water, whose sound suggested musical passages to him. This

experience led him to write the opening section of his famous *Ring* cycle of operas.

Rudyard Kipling tried not to think consciously but allowed his thoughts to drift, in effect turning off his left-brain editor and allowing his right brain full rein.

Henry Wadsworth Longfellow developed his ideas while sitting by the fire, the contemplative mood achieving a similar switch into right-brain thinking.

The writing of this chapter involved one of these break-through moments of my own. For a full day I wrestled with the direction it ought to take, the effort keeping me in left brain. It wasn't until I started to tidy my desk because I was due at a literary awards function that the ideas began to flow almost faster than I could scribble them down in note form. As soon as the pressure to write was removed the ideas began to come together.

The vital spark

Most of my writing at one time or another has depended on a Eureka moment, what some people call a sense of 'ah-ha', to give it the vital spark beyond mere craft.

My romance novel *Man and Wife* was born in a moment of hypnopompic (before fully awakening) reverie. I had been casting around for a new plot idea and had dropped the requirement like a letter into my mental mailbox before going to sleep. As I lay drowsing next morning I had a vision of a woman with a briefcase walking into a hallway and calling out, 'Darling, I'm home.' It was the sort of scene often shown in family TV shows but in my vision the roles were reversed. It was the *woman* who was coming home from the office to a welcome from a man. I began to wonder what would happen if a high-powered businesswoman hired a man to be her 'wife', providing her with the same kind of domestic back-up that most male business leaders enjoy.

Keeping a pad and pen by my bedside is routine now, so I scribbled the idea down and was surprised by its detail and complexity. In those few moments before fully awakening I had conceived almost the whole plot.

A short story, *Get out the Garamond*, anthologised in *A Ream of Writers* and later reprinted in a secondary school English textbook, was born in similar Eureka fashion. During the night I awoke with the story almost complete in my mind. It would be about an old-fashioned typesetter who keeps a certain typeface ready to announce the Second Coming of Christ, and what happens when the typeface is finally used.

The story came to me in such detail that plagiarism was a real concern. Later I was able to track the inspiration to its source, something we are rarely able to do, and found it was inspired by a joke I'd read a few days beforehand as part of some research.

My home study course in romance writing, which was later published as *The Art of Romance Writing*, came to me as a clear mental image of a ring binder containing many components. What they were I didn't know at the time, but I knew the folder would have fold-outs protruding from between the pages of the course itself. The logo of a heart rolling out of the platen of a typewriter came to me in the same vivid way.

Attracting the lightning

What all of these experiences have in common is that, while they may *seem* to strike like lightning out of the blue—and

187

indeed lightning is a common metaphor used when describing a Eureka experience—none of them comes without advance preparation.

It's as if the mind is a fertile field which needs to be tilled and seeded, then left for a while for the seed to germinate. I can't imagine Elias Howe dreaming of his sewing machine needle without first taking a keen interest in the sewing process itself. Archimedes had already considered the problem of the crown's composition before he entered his bath.

For myself, I'd toyed with the idea of producing a written guide to romance writing for many months. I had already written articles on the subject and taught a number of workshops. What eluded me until my Eureka moment was the precise form the course should take.

The writer Arthur Koestler called the process *bisociation*, the coming together of previously unrelated elements. The elements are placed in the melting pot of the mind, then left to simmer until they combine to form a previously undefined third element.

It seems as if we must first program the mental computer with as much information about the subject as we can, both directly and indirectly related to it. When you do this you set up the conditions necessary for the intuitive flash or Eureka moment to occur. In *The Intuitive Edge*, Philip Goldberg says, 'If you set out to pull a rabbit out of a hat, you will hardly be surprised when you perform that trick.'

So although the Eureka moment itself often comes as a surprise, what writer Marshall Cook calls 'a flash of summer lightning', there is a good chance you can prepare yourself to have these flashes more reliably. As Goldberg would put it, you simply provide yourself with a hat, take some lessons in basic magic and then go rabbit spotting.

There are four steps you can take to create a climate in which you are more likely to have these Eureka experiences. For easy recollection, they form the word SIFT, which stands for soak, incubate, flash and test.

Soak

This is akin to choosing hats and hunting for rabbits. Whatever your writing needs, you expose yourself to as many aspects of the problem as you can. Even if your reading isn't directly centred on the specific topic, read related material as long as it exposes your mind to many facets of the problem.

This is when the absorption trips described previously become valuable, exposing you to still more raw material for your idea factory. If you are simply seeking a good idea, absorption trips are the best way to open yourself to the widest range of possibilities.

Of course few writers want simply 'a good idea'. Most of us have a field of interest, whether it be science fiction, romance writing, how-to books or business writing. So, consciously or unconsciously, you will direct your investigations towards this area of general interest.

It's a good idea not to close off *any* avenue of exploration at this stage. Sometimes I get frustrated because I seem to be going off at tangents, reading old books or noodling through magazines with no apparent direction in mind. However, it's astonishing how often this apparently directionless reading takes me to some point of reference which will be helpful to me. Trust your subconscious mind. The editorial left brain will usually try to nag you into doing or reading something more 'useful', but it isn't always the best judge.

During the soak period, make a conscious effort to really see what's around you, instead of merely looking at it. The previous chapter sets out ways to soak up raw material. This is the time to put these methods into practice.

At the same time tell yourself that you expect to come up with the idea you need, or the solution to your writing problem. As the inventor Nikola Tesla expressed it, 'When natural inclination develops into a passionate desire, one advances towards his goal in seven-league boots.'

Incubate

This is possibly the hardest step to take because it feels so much like 'goofing off'. In effect this is just what you're telling your mind to do, providing it with some time and space in which to play with the raw materials you've fed into it.

The incubation period doesn't have to be one of total inactivity. It simply means you stop consciously working on a particular project. If you're writing a novel you could use the time to catch up on correspondence or professional reading. Sort out your filing system or your financial affairs. A different kind of writing may be beneficial, an article for a journal perhaps, or a proposal for another book entirely.

If you're incubating material for a non-fiction project, this may be the time to experiment with fiction or poetry, or some of the routine tasks that pile up while you're writing.

Other non-writing activities can also be done at this stage. Does the garden need weeding? The study need painting? These wordless pursuits may be the ideal way to busy your critical left brain while your right brain incubates the idea. Some writers also find exercise beneficial, whether it's walking, jogging or hang-gliding. The Concise Macquarie

190

dictionary defines *preoccupy* as 'to absorb or engross to the exclusion of other things' and that's what these activities are intended to do. By preoccupying your mind with other matters, you allow your idea factory to process the raw material with which you have primed it.

Flash

You will seldom be able to anticipate this moment and it almost never comes if you force it. I've lost count of the times I've pored over blank sheets of paper headed 'what if?' and 'why?' and gained no insight, only to have the solution to my writing problem present itself later that same evening during the 25th rerun of *M*A*S*H*.

Recently I was reading a decades-old book analysing the popularity of the TV series *Star Trek* when it came to me in a flash that the reasons behind the enduring popularity of the series might be the same as those behind the universal appeal of romance novels. This was a 'flash' that perfectly shows the SIFT formula at work. I had *soaked* in the subject matter simply because *Star Trek* is a hobby and romance writing is my living. Unknowingly I had *incubated* the material as I went about my writing career. It took the *flash* moment to put the two together, to perform one of Koestler's bisociations, his term for connections which are made outside normal awareness.

When the flash came I was totally relaxed, reading purely for pleasure (or so I thought). I had often wondered why romance novels are so enduringly popular, reasoning that millions of readers worldwide must gain more from them than mere entertainment or escapism, the usual explanations given. But nothing was further from my (conscious) mind as I

191

re-read that book about *Star Trek* and suddenly saw that the values espoused in the series and its later incarnations are the same as those embodied in romance novels. It was so obvious to me then that I wondered how I'd managed to miss it for so many years.

The felt sense

When it happens, a Eureka moment is unmistakable. Very often it involves a physical sensation, what Professor Eugene Gendlin of the University of Chicago calls a 'felt sense'. He and his colleagues studied tapes of hundreds of therapy sessions and discovered that successful therapy clients had a vague, hard-to-describe inner awareness which Gendlin called a 'felt sense' about their problems. Listening to the felt sense proved to be a key component of successful psychological change. Gendlin called the method of identifying the felt sense 'focusing'. He taught that paying attention to this 'bodily knowing' could lead to insight, physical release and positive life change. A felt sense can be as familiar as 'butterflies in the stomach' or a 'gut feeling' about the rightness of some decision. Some artists and writers when at their most creative have described physical sensations which correspond to the chakras, or energy centres of the body. But most creative people feel *some* physical sensation when experiencing a Eureka moment. Even if it's the first one you've ever had (or at least consciously noticed), you will recognise it because it usually provides at least the germ of an answer to a problem that has been on your mind, sometimes for days.

Often the answer will come at a moment when you're doing something completely unrelated to your writing work. You could be like Agatha Christie, doing the dishes, or driving, playing golf, showering, sleeping. Eureka moments frequently strike at highly inconvenient times. Many an artist has rushed away from a party to scribble down an idea that has struck in the middle of a conversation. It's no accident that whole plots, symphonies and advertising campaigns have been sketched out on table napkins in restaurants.

Capture the lightning

Unsociable as it may make you seem to others, it's essential to capture this 'summer lightning' as soon as it strikes. Any delay can see this vital insight vanish from your mind. I'm not sure why this happens but I know it does. For this reason I always carry a small notebook and pen and keep another by my bedside. When I have to spend an extended period in any of the four Bs—bed, bath, box or bus (to which you can add planes, trains and automobiles)—I make sure a notebook is kept near to hand.

Some of my best plotting has been done on international flights. I remember emptying a whole glass of red wine across a row of fellow passengers in the excitement of capturing an idea that came to me in the airspace over Hawaii.

Test

This is the final stage, when you hold the idea up to the light and see whether it is really as good as it seems. Some writers say that if you can't remember an idea without writing it down, it isn't that great to begin with. But I believe that we have so much on our minds these days it would take a very durable idea to survive without conscious recording.

If you find all sorts of left-brain injunctions intruding, you may have to go through the SIFT steps again. It may be your muse telling you that the idea isn't fully developed yet. This doesn't mean you shouldn't write while you still have *some* doubts. Most writers have doubts all the time. There's even a whole book describing the doubts that assail otherwise successful people. It's called *The Imposter Phenomenon, When Success Makes You Feel Like a Fake* by Dr Pauline Rose Clance (Peachtree, Georgia, 1985), and I commend it to you as an aid to overcoming these largely groundless fears and performance anxieties. The main thing is to teach yourself to distinguish between genuine doubts about the material and anxiety about your own ability to write it.

The test stage involves your editorial left brain, and this is the time to welcome your analytical side back. Put it to work examining the idea from all angles. Can this idea be combined with others? Can it be further developed to make it even better? But what about . . . ? And then there's . . . Just be sure that your left brain is working *with* the idea, not against it.

As *The Imposter Phenomenon* shows, there's a tendency to tell ourselves that if we had this idea, it can't possibly be any good. Scientists analysing Albert Einstein's notebooks found evidence that he first formulated his revolutionary 1916 general theory of relativity in 1913. His general theory, predicting that a planet's gravity creates the space and time that surround it, seemed so extraordinary to him at the time that he delayed publication because he feared he had insufficient justification for it.

It took the *test* stage to finally convince Einstein that he was right. He became convinced by irregularities in the orbit of Mercury and by an experiment during a solar eclipse in 1919—after he had published his theory—which showed that light beams from stars are 'bent' by the gravity of the sun.

While you may not start any revolutions, following the SIFT formula will almost certainly increase the number and quality of Eureka moments you experience. But don't stem the flow by expecting too much, too often. By their nature, Eureka moments are rare and special. Creative work has its own natural ebb and flow, which you must learn to accept and utilise. Even God took a day off after his six-day building project!

In a nutshell

1   Use the four Bs of inspiration—bed, bath, bus (or other transportation) and box (television) to free up your right brain while occupying your left brain.
2   Remember that Eureka moments come as sudden intuitive flashes—but not without advance preparation.
3   To have more Eureka moments, use the SIFT method:
    Soak yourself in background material, reading and studying all around the subject.
    Incubate, letting your mind play with the raw material while you do other things.
    Flash—be ready for the moment of inspiration and take note of it, but don't try to force it.
    Test—hold the idea up to the light, but don't expect all doubts to vanish before you start writing.

14

Your creative environment

Sooner or later every writer has to face the ordeal of moving from idea to written work. For some people this is such a terrifying prospect that they never get past it. Their novels will all be written 'someday', their articles and poems 'tomorrow'. But as we saw with Harry Hope in *The Iceman Cometh*, the problem with tomorrow and someday is that they never arrive.

Get rid of the idea that you will ever have the perfect mix of idea, setting and available time in which to create your masterwork. It will never happen.

It's probably a good idea to abandon the notion of a masterwork. All any writer can do is write their best work at any given moment. The readers decide its place, if any, in history. And the work that gets most acclaim probably won't be a lofty tome but some work you considered minor, probably written to a tight deadline or under financial pressure. That's the way it has always been throughout literary history. Everyone from William Shakespeare to Charles Dickens wrote to order. They would probably be astonished at the reverence accorded their work today.

My theory is that, of all my books, my romance novels would be the ones most likely to survive a global catastrophe. Not because they are literary masterpieces—neither of the above, in fact. But because a reader scurrying to shelter in the event of impending disaster is unlikely to snatch up an encyclopaedia to read in the dark hours ahead. It seems to me far more likely that she would grab the most comforting book to hand, her current romance title. And like the artifacts from Pompeii, the humble love story is what would rise phoenix-like from the ashes. Well, it's a nice thought anyway.

Budget your time

Earlier I established the importance of setting aside your most productive hours for writing. Even if you can only spare half an hour a day, it should become a regular commitment, like brushing your teeth.

If your schedule is especially tight, get into the habit of using the 'chinks' in it to plan, devise characters or solve plotting problems. You can write in your head while standing in a supermarket or bank queue, or busy your mind with characterisation in the dentist's waiting room. Carry a note-book with you everywhere to scribble down thoughts and ideas as they occur to you.

Your writing time should be kept for writing—putting words down one after the other on the page or screen. Talking about writing isn't writing. Thinking about writing isn't writing. Neither is changing a printer ribbon, photocopying reference material or playing 'what if' with a blank page. Your reserved writing time is precious. Treat it and yourself with respect, and try to fit in the other writing chores after the words are written.

Don't allow yourself to be sidetracked until you've completed a certain number of pages a day, although that number will depend on what feels right for you. Hemingway thought that wearing down seven No. 2 pencils was a measure of a good day's work. Somerset Maugham worked from nine to noon each day but produced 1000 words. Conrad was happy if he completed as little as a sentence in a day. Writing only two pages a day will give you a blockbuster-sized manuscript at the end of a year, and that's with most weekends off.

If the idea of producing a full-length manuscript seems daunting, focus instead on the words you plan to write *today*. If your target is two pages a day then all you need to worry about are those two pages.

A friend compares writing to running. The runner starts with a warm-up, working the muscles until they are comfortably warm. A writer starts by putting down the first trite thoughts that come to mind until the 'writing muscle' is sufficiently limber for full-on productivity. Like runners, writers get a second wind when inspired. Many are the days when I have all but given up around 4 p.m., only to find some stray thought catching my interest, whereupon I'll write like fury for the next couple of hours, long after I was supposedly 'written out' for the day.

Setting your writing goals

To achieve anything in life you need clearly defined goals, or at the very least a sense of direction. Writing goals are equally necessary. Why do you want to write? What do you most want to write about? What kind of writing appeals to you: articles, plays, poems, novels?

You may need to experiment with more than one form before deciding which suits you best. Many writers become proficient in several fields. Jeffrey Archer is not only a best-selling novelist but writes successful short stories as well. Colleen McCullough made her name with *The Thorn Birds*, then wrote everything from a cookbook to her multi-volume saga of the Roman Empire. The Australian crime writer Jennifer Rowe also writes award-winning children's books under the pen-name of Emily Rodda. There's no reason to limit yourself to one form of writing if you find several that suit your talents and interests.

The crucial requirement is to finish what you start. Beginning a science fiction story, then abandoning it in favour of a romance novel, and that for a play, is a kind of 'creative procrastination'. It's a way of putting off the test of manuscript submission by never finishing anything.

If you have a good idea for a second project while working on the first, jot down the essentials and file them for later attention. As well as making a deal with yourself to produce a certain number of pages a day, resolve also to finish what you start, at least in the beginning. Later you will develop the judgment to know when a project should be abandoned, but it doesn't happen all that often, although the temptation is often there. For now, resolve to see each project through to the finish.

Invest in your craft

Away from the typewriter, invest in yourself and your craft. Writing is a business like any other, and requires not only time but also money for subscriptions to professional journals and membership of writers' organisations, as well as stationery and postage.

During your absorption trips you'll incur fares and expenses, although these trips may be combined with everyday social outings. Purchasing a variety of newspapers and magazines for raw materials costs money, although you can pool these with other writer friends to share the cost. But it is all money well spent if you are committed to writing rather than 'being a writer'. The latter involves almost no cost at all as you will spend all your time at parties and social gatherings discussing the work you are going to write, but of course never do. As we concluded earlier, there is no harm in this provided you are honest with yourself. You will save yourself a lot of time, heartache and expense by deciding at the outset that you will enjoy writing as a hobby.

Once you decide to *write*, as distinct from being a writer, and once you know what form your writing will take, you can set out on your absorption trips, read widely in your area of interest and beyond, and fill your idea factory with raw materials.

Until now you've built castles in the air, but now it's time, as Thoreau said, to put foundations under them. We've already looked at why many people don't achieve their writing goals. The main reasons are lack of real interest and fear of failure, as well as fear of actual loss. Committing yourself to your writing goals gets rid of the first block. Fear of failure will probably always be with you in some form, but you can resolve to write in spite of the doubts that assail you.

The paddling duck syndrome

In workshops I tell the story of the paddling duck, because it is surprising how few writers realise that they are not the only ones who feel insecure about their work. It started when I began to learn to play the piano and found I have no musical aptitude whatsoever. But learning is fun and I'm fulfilling a lifelong fantasy, and I'm not planning on playing at the Opera House any time soon. What does matter is the lesson about writing I have learned from the experience.

For years I harboured a fantasy of my fingers rippling effortlessly over the keyboard as I produced wonderful music. It's not only my lack of aptitude that has shown me that this is a fantasy. No matter how skilled I become with diligent practice and no matter how effortless my playing looks to *others*, I will always be aware of the mechanics involved. The outward image and the inner experience will always be at odds.

This may explain why every professional writer, artist or performer secretly envies all the others. They think that they are alone in their struggle with the muse, while all the others apparently possess the secret of seamless performance.

The truth is, *all artists feel this way*. No matter how skilled they are, they remain aware of the craft underlying the art. The dancer floating across the stage feels every straining muscle; the writer whose work is admired for its fluency is conscious of all the drafts that went into the published work.

As the Sydney radio personality Brian Bury described it

while interviewing me, 'It's like the duck sailing across the water. Above the water line everything is serene but underneath he's paddling like crazy.'

Striving to reach the unreachable only leads to frustration, and it can dry up the creative well altogether if you let it. Like the duck who always knows what his feet are doing beneath the surface, a writer must take what comfort he can in making the work *appear* seamless to others, knowing it will never feel that way inside—as it never does to any creative person. The important thing is to keep on paddling.

The work destroyers

Hemingway called the telephone and visitors 'the work destroyers'. Worry also destroyed his ability to write, as did ill health when it produced worry.

If you strongly wish to write, then you will make the effort to screen out such distractions. Jane Austen wrote in the middle of family activities. Anthony Trollope wrote while travelling to and from his job at the post office, while William Faulkner wrote on the job in the boiler room of a power plant. Most of the excuses that stop you from writing must be recognised for what they are—excuses.

There will be times when your children need you or you have legitimate community or social commitments. But—and this is a big but—if writing is important to you, you will make time for it. If you are truly unable to find even half an hour a day in which to write then you should probably re-examine your level of commitment. However noble it may sound to be a writer who is kept from the muse by duty and responsibility, it is very rarely the whole truth. Like the writer who was able to take his dog to obedience classes despite writing a daily newspaper column, there is always time for the things we truly want to do.

Time has a lot in common with money: there is never enough of it. But what happens when you incur a parking fine? Somehow you find the money to pay it, mostly because it beats going to jail or losing your licence. Whether you take the money from some other purpose or use a credit card is beside the point. The money is found. Time can be found on the same basis, by taking it from somewhere else: sacrificing some television viewing or an hour's sleep in the morning. Where there's a will, there is always a way.

Inner distractions

Less easy to dismiss are the distractions that arise from within. It is these that often drive us to *welcome* the sound of the doorbell or telephone even as we complain about them, because it gives us an excuse to avoid facing our inner demons.

'Every act of creation is first of all an act of destruction,' Pablo Picasso said. Mixed in with the joy of creation there is nearly always some uncertainty—will I be good enough; will I make a fool of myself; isn't it self-indulgent, writing when others need me?

Remember, the most creative people are those who first *believe* they are creative. Get rid of any stereotype you may have of a writer as a particular kind of person. During a television interview for the *Today* show a young would-be writer observed that I didn't *look* like a romance writer. He wanted to write romance novels, but hadn't thought to look in a mirror to see if he measured up to his own stereotype! Writers aren't necessarily thin, tortured or of any particular age. Tim Winton published his first novel in his teens. Historian Nance Irvine is still writing in her eighties.

Change your self talk

If you still find yourself plagued by self-doubts about the appropriateness of what you're trying to do or about the worth of yourself and your ideas, try Barry Watts's remedy and 'catch yourself thinking'. Replace the negative thoughts with positive ones. These are called *affirmations* and they are simply goals in written form, phrased as if they were already an accomplished fact.

Affirmations are used to get messages past your editorial left brain and into your right brain, where they become part of your thinking. Psychologists call the messages we give ourselves *self talk*. It's the chatter that goes on in our heads so persistently that most of the time we're unaware of it until we make a deliberate effort to quiet it through relaxation or meditation. Even then it keeps starting up again, requiring constant work to subdue it or change the messages.

You can change your self talk so it becomes helpful to you rather than hindering your efforts. Affirmations should be positive and encouraging, and written as if they were already fact. Your mind can't distinguish between an imagined event and one that really happened, so by writing your affirmations in present tense, as if they already exist, you can fool your idea factory into believing them.

I write my affirmations on small slips of paper and place them in desk and dressing table drawers, on the bathroom mirror, anywhere I'm likely to come across them several times a day.

204

When you write affirmations, use personal pronouns: I, me, mine. 'I enjoy writing' rather than 'writing is a worthwhile activity'.

Others you might try are:

I have more ideas than I can use.
My writing improves with every day.
Ideas come easily to me.
My characters live in my mind and on the page.
My words move the world.

It doesn't matter whether or not you believe the affirmations at first. By sending these messages to your subconscious on a regular basis and dismissing any negative thoughts the moment they creep into your mind, you are in effect *programming* your subconscious to act on the statements as if they were already fact.

Like visualising and mental practice, affirmations are a kind of drill, a mental aerobics which can help to develop the writing muscles you desire.

A few years ago I had the privilege of meeting Neil Armstrong when he visited Australia. His charm and gentle humour were enormously impressive for someone who, to me, is a modern-day Columbus. His first words as he set foot on the moon are engraved into our collective memories: 'That's one small step for [a] man . . . one giant leap for mankind.' Dr Denis Waitley, who has worked with the NASA astronauts, documents that Armstrong later added, 'It was just like we planned it . . . just like drill.' Affirmations are the drill you can use to change your self talk from negative to positive and achieve your writing ambitions. Affirmations can take you from where you are now to any place you can imagine. In Armstrong's case it was all the way to the moon.

Dear diary,today I reached the moon...

If you truly believe, what might you too achieve?

The extra leg

Everybody's idea factory goes on strike now and then. But there are a number of things you can do to get the creative juices flowing again. Remember Grenville's Law: it can all be fixed tomorrow. Nothing you write today is graven in stone. A painting by Rembrandt in the Louvre in Paris shows a figure on a horse and is notable because the horse has five legs. The extra leg is a phantom, created when the master changed the position of the horse. But the original pose is still visible beneath the layers of paint. If it was okay for Rembrandt to experiment till he got it right then you have no need to be ashamed of doing successive drafts to achieve your writing aims.

In the meantime, there are five steps you can take to free up your creativity when you get stuck.

1   *Write for yourself alone*
    Create a draft that no-one will be allowed to see. Allow yourself to get in touch with all your memories and feelings, painful and joyful alike, and write them into the work. Drop your guard. Know that this draft is for your eyes only, for now anyway.

2   *Write for the fun of it*
    Remember *sanuk*? If your work doesn't provide you with *sanuk* (fun and joy), how can it possibly entertain or inspire anyone else? Write to say whatever it is you want to say rather than to impress a boss, editor or publisher. Writing to impress is a sure way to set yourself up to fail, because you make success or your reputation more important than the work itself.

3   *Set deadlines for yourself but be gentle*
    Every time you miss a writing appointment with yourself you tell your idea factory that the writing is optional. Your mind gets the message that writing isn't your priority, so it gets harder and harder for you to sit down and work. Spend the agreed time at your desk even when things aren't going well and tell your subconscious that you can and will do this, it's only a matter of time. Be realistic in setting deadlines. Setting a target of two pages a day and producing them is better than aiming for a chapter a day and failing.

4   *Respect your work*
    How can you expect others to respect your writing time if you don't? Each time you drop what you're writing to

answer a family summons (other than a genuine emergency), you send the message that you are interruptible. I find it helps to say I'm *working* rather than *writing*, as this helps to make the point. Unfortunately many people don't consider writing to be 'real work', so it's up to you to show that it is. As in all facets of life, actions speak louder than words.

5   *Finish what you start*
Just as many journalists I know have an unfinished novel in their desk drawer, the world is full of people who intend to start writing 'someday'. When you abandon a project midway, you send a negative message to your right brain. You show that you aren't serious about this activity. By finishing what you start, even when it's going badly, you reinforce your self-image as an achiever. You've finished the article, poem or play. You *are* creative. You *can* do this.

Above all, adopt a creative attitude to life. Believe in your own abilities and trust that belief to make it fact. Remember that creative people:

- experience life in all its richness
- refuse to accept any limitations, whether physical, cultural, age or gender-based
- appreciate the unusual, seek out the different
- love to play and enjoy word games, puzzles and diversions, which bring out their inner child
- consider themselves unique, never comparing themselves to others. As the *Desiderata* says, 'Always there will be greater and lesser persons than yourself.'

Take to heart the words of Thomas Wolfe in *The Web and the Rock*:

If we have a talent and cannot use it, we have failed. If we have a talent and use only half of it, we have partly failed. If we have a talent and learn somehow to use all of it, we have gloriously succeeded and won a satisfaction and a triumph few individuals ever know.

In a nutshell

1 Stop waiting for the perfect mix of idea, setting and available time—start writing anyway.
2 Save your best writing time for actual writing, putting words on paper. Only worry about what you have to write *today*.
3 Finish what you start.
4 Be prepared to invest in your writing.
5 Remember the paddling duck—try to make the work look effortless to others while accepting that it will never feel that way to you.
6 Examine inner and outer distractions in the light of your commitment to your writing. We make time for the things we really want to do.
7 Use positive affirmations to change your self talk and reprogram your idea factory.
8 Write for the *sanuk* (joy) of it and you'll communicate that joy to others.

Bibliography

Ashe, Geoffrey, *The Art of Writing Made Simple*, Chaucer Press, London, 1972, pp. 22–3

Beaumont, J. Graham, ed., *Brainpower: Unlock the Power of Your Mind*, Andromeda Oxford, Oxford, 1989

Beaumont, Joanna, *How You Can Make $25 000 a Year From Writing in Australia and New Zealand*, Orlando Press, Sydney, 1986, p. 9

Berry, Adrian, 'Einstein relatively feary', *The Daily Telegraph Mirror*, Sydney, 21 October 1994, p. 32

Birmingham, Frederic A., *The Writer's Craft*, Arthur Barker, London, 1959, pp. 278–79

Block, Lawrence, *Telling Lies for Fun and Profit*, Arbor House, New York, 1981

Blythe, Hal, and Sweet, Charlie, 'Collaborwriting', *The 1989 Novel & Short Story Writer's Market*, Henry, Laurie, ed., Writer's Digest Books, Ohio, 1989, pp. 53–55

Botkin, James W., Mahdi Elmandjra and Mircea Malitza, *No Limits to Learning, Bridging the Human Gap*, Pergamon, London, 1979, pp. 12–13

Bradbury, Ray, 'The thing at the top of the stairs', *How to Write Tales of Horror, Fantasy and Science Fiction*, Williamson, J.N. ed., Writer's Digest Books, Ohio, 1987

Bristol, Claude M., *The Magic of Believing, The Science of Setting Your Goal . . . and Then Reaching It!*, Cornerstone Library, New York, 1969

Burn, Helen, memo, Centre for Public Broadcasting, Division of Programming and Operations, Maryland, 26 May 1972

Carnegie, Dale, *How to Win Friends and Influence People*, Simon and Schuster, New York, 1939

Clance, Dr Pauline Rose, *The Imposter Phenomenon, When Success Makes You Feel Like a Fake*, Bantam, Atlanta, 1985

Coghlan, Sandy, *Insight into Chakras and Colours*, Pegasus Education Group, Melbourne, 1994

—— ed., *Museletter*, Melbourne, Issue No. 8, July/August 1994

Cook, Marshall, 'Training your muse: seven steps to harnessing your creativity', *Writer's Digest*, Ohio, March 1986, pp. 26–30

Cussler, Clive, *Raise the Titanic*, Viking Press, New York, 1976

de Bono, Edward, *de Bono's Thinking Course*, Facts on File, New York, 1982

—— *PO: Beyond Yes & No*, Simon & Schuster, New York, 1972, pp. 56–64

Downey, Bill, *Right Brain . . . Write On! Overcoming Writer's Block and Achieving your Creative Potential*, Prentice-Hall, New York, 1984

Drake, Mary, *The Trees Were Green, Memories of Growing Up After the Great War*, Hale & Iremonger, Sydney, 1984

Dyer, Wayne, *How to Be a No-Limit Person*, audiocassette, The Seminar Company, 1994

Edwards, Betty, *Drawing on the Artist Within, How to Release Your Hidden Creativity*, Fontana, London, 1987, pp. 24–6, 143, 205

—— *Drawing on the Right Side of the Brain*, J.P. Tarcher, Los Angeles, 1979

Finney, Barbara, 'Writing for fun: a magical jar of self esteem', *Writer's Digest*, Ohio, June 1987, pp. 34–5

Gawain, Shakti, *Creative Visualisation*, Bantam, New York, 1978

Geiselmann, R.E., Fisher, R.P., Mackinnon, D.P. and Holland, H.L., 'Enhancement of eyewitness memory with the cognitive interview', *American Journal of Psychology*, No. 99, Los Angeles, 1986, pp. 385–401

Gendlin, Gene, *Focusing*, Bantam, New York, 1981

Gerrold, David, *The Trouble with Tribbles*, Ballantine, New York, 1973, pp. 148–49

211

—— *The World of Star Trek*, Ballantine, New York, 1979

Goldberg, Philip, *The Intuitive Edge, Understanding Intuition and Applying It in Everyday Life*, J.P. Tarcher, Los Angeles, 1983, pp. 63–6, 165–69, 179

Goldman, William, *Adventures in the Screen Trade*, Futura, London and Sydney, 1984, pp. 319, 400

Gray, Ginna, *Coming Home*, Romantic Times, New York, June/July 1989, p. 85

Hanks, Kurt, Belliston, Larry and Edwards, Dave, *Design Yourself*, William Kaufmann, Los Altos CA, 1977

Harman, Willis and Rheingold, Howard, *Higher Creativity, Liberating the Unconscious for Breakthrough Insights*, J.P. Tarcher, Los Angeles, 1984

Harris, Thomas, *I'm OK, You're OK*, Pan, London, 1970

Hathaway, Nancy, '15 great creative block-busters', *New Woman*, June 1987, pp. 54–8

Hill, Napoleon, *Think and Grow Rich*, Fawcett Publications, Greenwich Conn, 1960

Huddle, David, 'The writing habit', *The 1989 Novel & Short Story Writer's Market*, Henry, Laurie, ed., Writer's Digest Books, Ohio, 1989

Jameson, Julietta, 'Hearing aids to help you speak', *The Daily Telegraph Mirror*, Sydney, 17 October 1994, p. 32

Jones, Andrea, 'Map of the human mind', *The Sun Herald*, Sydney, 26 June 1994, p. 140

Kelly, Martin, 'Work skills "out of date in 3 years"', *The Daily Telegraph Mirror*, Sydney, 15 May 1989, p. 3

Konicov, Barry, *Chakra Meditation*, audiocassette, Potentials Unlimited, Michigan, 1988

Lichtenberg, Jacqueline, Marshak, Sondra and Winston, Joan, *Star Trek Lives*, Corgi, London, 1975

Long, George, trans., *The Meditations of Marcus Aurelius, A Practical Guide for Living in an Irrational World*, Avon, New York, 1993, pp. 84, 86

McCullough, Colleen, *The Thorn Birds*, Harper & Row, New York, 1977

MacGregor, Sandy, *Piece of Mind*, Creative Accelerated Learning Methods, Sydney, 1992

Mack, Karin and Skjei, Eric, *Overcoming Writing Blocks*, J.P. Tarcher, Los Angeles, 1979

McKisson, *Chrysalis, Nurturing Creative and Independent Thought in Children*, Zephyr Press, Tucson Arizona, 1981

Mackenzie, R. Alec, *The Time Trap, How to Get More Done in Less Time*, McGraw-Hill, New York, 1975

Maltz, Maxwell, *Creative Living for Today*, Simon & Schuster, New York, 1972

Manners, William, 'Write prolifically in your spare time', *The 1989 Novel & Short Story Writer's Market*, Henry, Laurie, ed., Writer's Digest Books, Ohio, 1989, pp. 41–8

Meyer, Paul J., 'How to direct your life', *SMI World News*, Success Motivation Institute, Melbourne, Third Quarter 1989

Mills & Boon, 'Ever thought of writing a romance?' tip sheet, *Mills & Boon*, London, 1982

Nierenberg, Gerard I., *The Art of Creative Thinking*, Simon & Schuster, New York, 1982

Nimoy, Leonard, *I am not Spock*, Celestial Arts, Milbrae CA, 1975, pp. 118, 137

O'Reilly, Robert J., *Dynamic Thinking*, Prentice-Hall, New Jersey, 1963

Parv, Valerie, *Think Slim, Be Trim*, Rigby, Adelaide, 1981, pp. 23–8

—— 'Get out the Garamond', *A Ream of Writers*, Yorke, Susan, ed., Society of Women Writers (Australia), NSW Branch, Sydney, 1982

—— *Man and Wife*, Mills & Boon, London, 1984

—— *Man Shy*, Mills & Boon, 1987

—— 'A muddled system of trial and error', *The Writer's News*, Cromarty Press, Narrabeen, February 1987, p. 21

—— 'How many in your quartet, Mr Brubeck?', *The Writer's News*, March 1987, p. 11

—— 'When no muse is good news', *The Writer's News*, April 1987, p. 11

—— 'Be a bard-of-all-trades', *The Writer's News*, May 1987, p. 11

—— 'Right brain, right idea', *The Writer's News*, June 1987, p. 11

—— 'Treading where no writer has trod before', *The Writer's News*, July 1987, pp. 13–14

—— 'Reading the write act', *The Writer's News*, August 1987, pp. 11–12

—— 'Prodded into prosperity, on the care and feeding of editors . . .', *The Writer's News*, September 1987, pp. 11–12

—— *Centrefold*, Mills & Boon, 1988

—— *Man Without a Past*, Mills & Boon 1988

—— *That Midas Man*, Mills & Boon 1990

—— *Innovative Learning, the key to higher creativity*, bachelor's thesis, September 1990

—— *A Fair Exchange*, Mills & Boon, 1991

—— *Island of Dreams*, Mills & Boon, 1992

—— *The Art of Romance Writing, How to create, write and sell your contemporary romance novel,* Allen & Unwin, Sydney, 1993

—— *Sister of the Bride*, Mills & Boon, 1996

—— *A Royal Romance*, Mills & Boon, 1996

Phillips, Larry W., ed., *Ernest Hemingway on Writing*, Collins, London, 1984, p. 34

Plimpton, George, ed., *Writers at Work, The Paris Review Interviews*, second series, Penguin, New York, 1963, pp. 167–191, 222–223

Rico, Gabriele Lusser, *Writing the Natural Way*, J.P. Tarcher, Los Angeles, 1983

Roddenberry, Gene, *The Literary View of the Future*, audiocassette, World Future Society, Washington DC, 1984

Rogers, Carl, *On Becoming a Person*, Houghton-Mifflin, Boston, 1961

Sackett, Susan, Goldstein, Fred and Goldstein, Stan, *Star Trek Speaks*, Pocket Books, New York, 1979

Safe, Mike, 'The best-selling WHAMWASH from Bondi', *The Australian Magazine*, Sydney, 30 January 1993, pp. 20–26

Shanks, Bob, *Drop-out Father*, feature film directed by Don Taylor, CBS Entertainment, Los Angeles and New York, 1982

Speer, Flora, 'Mini Profile', *Romantic Times*, New York, June/July 1989, p. 85

Stearn, Jess, *The Power of Alpha Thinking*, New American Library, New York, 1976

Strunk, Jr., William and White, E.B., *The Elements of Style*, third edition, Macmillan, New York, 1979

Sturgeon, Theodore, 'Shore Leave', *Star Trek* TV script, directed by Robert Sparr, Desilu, Los Angeles, airdate 29 December 1966

—— 'Future writer in a future world', *The Craft of Science Fiction*, Brettnor, R., ed., Harper & Row, New York, 1976, p. 89

Sunholm, Trisha, 'The write way to success', *The Writer's News*, Cromarty Press, Sydney, March 1990, pp. 16–17

Theodore, Des, 'Keeping notes', 'Learning from marketing', unpublished correspondence, 1994

Toffler, Alvin, *Future Shock*, Pan, London, 1971, pp. 418–425

Ueland, Brenda, 'The imagination works slowly and quietly', *The 1989 Novel & Short Story Writer's Market* Henry, Laurie, ed., Writer's Digest Books, Ohio, 1989, pp. 23–27

Van Den Nieuwenhof, Liz, 'Kids forget how to play', *The Sunday Telegraph*, Sydney, 26 June 1994, p. 41

Von Oech, Roger, *A Whack on the Side of the Head*, Warner, New York, 1983

Waitley, Denis, *Seeds of Greatness, The Ten Best-kept Secrets of Total Success*, Heinemann, London, 1983, pp. 54–63

Wallace, Irving, *The Writing of One Novel*, NEL, London, 1969

Waterhouse, Keith, 'You call this work', *Moneycare*, National Westminster Bank, London, August 1984, pp. 12–13

Watts, Barry and Coghlan, Sandy, *Creative Thinking* audiocassettes, Pegasus Educational Group, Melbourne, 1994

Weinberg, Dr George, *Self Creation*, Futura, London, 1978

Weiser Cornell, Ann, *The Focusing Student's Manual*, third edition, Focusing Resources, Berkeley CA, 1994

Wolfe, Thomas, *The Web and the Rock*, Harper Bros, New York and London, 1939

World Future Society, 'Outlook for '89 and beyond', *The Futurist*, Washington DC, November–December 1988, p. 54

Index

right-brain thinking, 14, 17,
27, 34–48 *passim*
Right Brain, Write On
(Downey), 35
Ring cycle of operas, 186
Roddenberry, Gene, 50, 150
Rogers, Carl, 55
Rowe, Jennifer (Emily
Rodda), 199
Royal Romance, A (Parv), 71,
181

Sanders, Colonel Harland, 107
sanuk, 13, 14, 17, 18, 20, 51,
117, 157, 207, 209
saturation, 103, 173; trap,
104, 114
scenes, writing in, 148
Schindler's Ark (Keneally), 59
seeing, new ways of, 21, 25,
69
selection of ideas, 121–2, 128,
137
self-publishing, 11, 86
self-talk, 49, 51, 53, 204
sensory impressions, 154
sequence trap, the, 105, 115,
123, 126, 164
Shakespeare, 170, 196
Shaw, Bernard, 176
SIFT process, 189–95
signature test, 30
Silhouette Books, 82
Sister of the Bride (Parv), 71
sleep, 158–66 *passim*; synthesis,
165

slush pile, 7
Smith, Wilbur, 168
soak, *see* SIFT process
Society of Women Writers,
179
soft data, 167, 177
specific, 78–9, 121, 132
Speer, Flora, 169
Star Trek, 50, 53, 191–2
states of consciousness, *see* sleep
stream-of-consciousness, 28
Sturgeon, Theodore, 6; *see
also* matter
Summer of the Seventeenth Doll
(Lawler), 89
Sunday Telegraph, 41
survey the problem, 120, 128
synopsis, *see* outline

techniques of good writing, 2
Tesla, Nikola, 190
test, *see* SIFT process
theme, 12
Theodore, Des, 1, 62–3
theta, 160; *see also* brainwave
activity
Think and Grow Rich (Hill), 55
Thoreau, 200
Thorn Birds, The
(McCullough), 179, 198
thought switches, 31, 49
time, budgeting, 197, 207;
shortage of , 84–5
Toffler, Alvin, 8–9, 14, 74
tomorrowitis, 111–12, 115
Transactional Analysis, 92, 99